Building Community Resilience to Large Oil Spills

Findings and Recommendations from a Synthesis
of Research on the Mental Health, Economic,
and Community Distress Associated with the
Deepwater Horizon Oil Spill

MELISSA L. FINUCANE, AARON CLARK-GINSBERG, ANDREW M. PARKER,
ALEJANDRO U. BECERRA-ORNELAS, NOREEN CLANCY,
RAJEEV RAMCHAND, TIM SLACK, VANESSA PARKS, LYNSAY AYER,
AMANDA F. EDELMAN, ELIZABETH L. PETRUN SAYERS,
SHANTHI NATARAJ, CRAIG A. BOND, AMY E. LESEN,
REGARDT J. FERREIRA, LEAH DRAKEFORD, JACQUELINE FIORE,
MARGARET M. WEDEN, K. BRENT VENABLE, A. BARRIE BLACK

Sponsored by the Gulf of Mexico Research Initiative

For more information on this publication, visit www.rand.org/t/RRA409-1

Library of Congress Cataloging-in-Publication Data is available for this publication.
ISBN: 978-1-9774-0535-7

Published by the RAND Corporation, Santa Monica, Calif.
© Copyright 2020 RAND Corporation
RAND® is a registered trademark.

Cover: Johannes Schmitt-Tegge/dpa/Alamy Live News.

Support RAND
Make a tax-deductible charitable contribution at
www.rand.org/giving/contribute

www.rand.org

Preface

Ten years after the 2010 Deepwater Horizon oil spill, policymakers and practitioners are eager to know what has been learned from research on the mental health, economic, and community distress associated with the disaster in the Gulf of Mexico. In this report, we briefly summarize and synthesize key findings from relevant research and identify recommendations for improving community resilience to another large oil spill. The report presents guidance for diverse stakeholders interested in supporting communities affected by and recovering from oil spills. This report will be informative for members of government agencies responsible for disaster preparedness, response, and recovery; nongovernmental organizations working to improve community resilience; local community leaders working directly with coastal residents whose livelihoods depend on natural resources; private-sector companies involved in reducing risk; and scientists and donors (federal and private) responsible for distributing resources that support research in this field.

Community Health and Environmental Policy Program

RAND Social and Economic Well-Being is a division of the RAND Corporation that seeks to actively improve the health and social and economic well-being of populations and communities throughout the world. This research was conducted in the Community Health and Environmental Policy Program within RAND Social and Economic Well-Being. The program focuses on such topics as infrastructure, science and technology, community design, community health promotion, migration and population dynamics, transportation, energy, and climate and the environment, as well as other policy concerns that are influenced by the natural and built environment, technology, and community organizations and institutions that affect well-being. For more information, email chep@rand.org.

Funding

Funding for this research was provided by a grant from the Gulf of Mexico Research Initiative (grant #231501-00), and gifts from RAND supporters and income from operations. Data are publicly available through the Gulf of Mexico Research Initiative Information and Data Cooperative at https://data.gulfresearchinitiative.org (doi: 10.7266/N76971Z0, 10.7266/1D4HS43N, 10.7266/6QDWMGMK, 10.7266/n7-h9ty-ce44).

Contents

Figures

Tables

Summary

The 2010 Deepwater Horizon (DWH) oil spill was the largest in U.S. history, releasing an estimated 4.9 million barrels of oil into the Gulf of Mexico.[1] The scale of the disaster motivated diverse stakeholders to examine the human dimensions of the spill and how communities' resilience to similar threats could be improved. This examination is needed because, as long as humans depend on extracting oil and gas for energy, coastal regions are at risk for spills. In this report, we explore how communities, government officials, nongovernmental organizations, businesses, and scientists can build community resilience to large oil spills.

In addition to paying more than $20.8 billion in environmental damages, BP allocated $500 million to establish the Gulf of Mexico Research Initiative (GoMRI) to distribute funds for independent research. About 4.2 percent of the GoMRI funding awarded through the competitive grant process (approximately $16.8 million of $400 million) was allocated to scientific studies of behavioral and socioeconomic impacts, population health, environmental risk assessment, and community capacity considerations (theme 5).[2] A small but growing body of empirical work is emerging on the mental health, economic, and social aspects of the DWH spill on Gulf Coast communities. However, there has been no comprehensive synthesis of these studies. Moreover, the implications of those findings have yet to be distilled into specific recommendations for various stakeholder groups. In this report, we aim to

- identify key findings from research on the human dimensions of the DWH oil spill, particularly related to mental health, economic, and community distress
- provide recommendations, based on extant research, for improving Gulf Coast communities' ability to deal with the risks of a large oil spill.

We examined peer-reviewed articles and other reports published from 2010 through 2019 from diverse social science fields, topics, methods, populations, periods, and geographies. Relevant documents were identified via a topic search of "Deepwater Horizon" in Web of Science, PubMed, and other online databases specific to disasters or to the DWH oil spill. Although physical and mental health are closely related within the disaster context, our literature review for this report did not include studies that primarily examined physical health impacts. Other reports synthesizing research on physical health impacts are available; the narrower focus in this report reflects the authors' expertise and the specific objectives of the funding allocated.[3]

---

[1] U.S. Coast Guard and National Response Team, 2011.

[2] Personal communication with GoMRI officials.

[3] Aguilera et al., 2010; Kwok, Engel, et al., 2017; Eklund et al., 2019; Laffon, Pásaro, and Valdiglesias, 2016.

Initial results of the literature review were presented to representatives of nongovernment organizations, academic researchers, and community leaders who attended a workshop in New Orleans on February 8, 2019.

Our review of the literature identified mixed evidence of distress associated with the DWH disaster and a variety of factors that affected the nature and severity of people's experiences. Key findings from the research are shown in Table S.1.

Table S.1. Key Research Findings

Mental Health Distress

- Diverse studies provide mixed evidence for short- and long-term mental health distress (depression, anxiety, and posttraumatic stress) associated with the DWH oil spill.

- Life disruption (particularly income loss), prior trauma, and various sociodemographic characteristics were important drivers of negative mental health symptoms.

- Higher levels of social capital—particularly social support, sense of community, and perceived resiliency—had a protective impact against spill-related stress, except for groups with high attachment to damaged resources (e.g., fishing households).

- Some social groups reported experiencing more distress than others, partly because of the differing levels and types of prior trauma, disruption from the oil spill, or available support.

Economic Impacts

- Economic losses from the DWH oil spill were limited to the short term for the commercial fishing, oil and gas, and tourism industries. However, years after the oil spill, high proportions of households reported very negative impacts on their financial situations.

- The most-severe economic impacts were reported by poorer households.

- Aggregate analyses by industry showed that unemployment rates were not permanently affected by the spill.

- Economic impacts were highly heterogenous, with a net increase in employment and wages in some areas (e.g., in Louisiana, in part because of the resources needed for spill clean-up) but a decline in employment and wages in other areas (e.g., Florida).

Community Distress

- Conditions following the DWH oil spill were consistent with an environment that would negatively impact community well-being by reducing trust in authorities, weakening social networks, increasing perceptions of inequitable distribution of post-spill resources, and increasing domestic violence.

- Substantial percentages of coastal households (e.g., nearly 38 percent of an Alabama sample) were involved directly or indirectly in some type of claims, settlement, or litigation activity associated with the DWH oil spill, thereby prolonging the recovery process. Uncertainty over the extent of oil spill impacts, competing narratives of responsibility and blame, protracted litigation and compensation processes, and perceptions of injustice related to these factors were chronic stressors.

- Communities were variably positioned in terms of vulnerability (e.g., fishing dependence) and resilience (e.g., social capital and community attachment).

- Different groups demonstrated different experiences of loss and recovery. Fishing households, in particular, reported high levels of DWH-related disruption of social routines.

During the literature review and workshop discussions, several themes emerged regarding ways to reduce the stress of large oil spills and build resilience to catastrophic events. These multifaceted themes formed the basis of several key recommendations, as shown in Table S.2.

The recommendations reflect discussions with workshop participants about the findings from the literature review and are intended for implementation *before* the next large oil spill.

Table S.2. Summary of Recommendations

Recommendation	Stakeholders with Primary Role
• **Focus on the needs of people and their communities.**	
○ Address acute needs (e.g., train and place community health workers to build local capacity for disaster response).	Government (all levels), NGOs
○ Ensure ongoing local support (e.g., provide sustained resources to local programs to address social disparities).	Local government, NGOs, private sector
○ Identify and support vulnerable populations (e.g., ensure that fishers have access to alternative livelihoods or income).	Local government, NGOs, private sector, scientists
• **Address the complexity of the resource-dependent social systems in which disasters are managed.**	
○ Centralize social science in systems-based approaches to risk management (e.g., use citizen science to identify community assets for emergency response plans).	Federal government, scientists
○ Ensure that diverse information can be integrated by communities thinking holistically about their long-term needs and goals (e.g., provide funds to encourage communities to identify priority goals and strategies for achieving them).	Government (all levels), NGOs, scientists
○ Improve claims processes (e.g., clarify procedures in determining payouts ahead of the next disaster).	Federal government, private sector, scientists
• **Enhance partnerships, leveraging diverse sets of skills and strengths.**	
○ Work with local partners (e.g., engage residents in disaster citizen science).	Government (all levels), NGOs, private sector, scientists
○ Leverage diverse skills to build systems-level capacity (e.g., use telemedicine to provide tailored, time-sensitive mental health care).	Federal government, NGOs, scientists
○ Integrate diverse perspectives through collaborations (e.g., enhance links between researchers and local residents through formal arrangements with community health workers).	Government (all levels), NGOs, private sector, scientists
• **Connect the past, present, and future contexts to support disaster recovery efforts.**	
○ Examine extant policies and practices for ways to reduce vulnerabilities and increase resilience (e.g., identify potential hazardous waste disposal sites before the next disaster to distribute risk across sociodemographic groups).	Government (all levels), NGOs, private sector, scientists
○ Improve adaptive capacity through preparedness and diversification (e.g., provide guidance to households about how to prepare for the mental, economic, and social distress associated with an oil spill).	Government (all levels), private sector

Recommendation	Stakeholders with Primary Role
• **Deepen the evidence base for building community resilience.**	
○ Partner with communities through participatory research approaches (e.g., partner with local organizations to design surveys and collect information).	Federal government, NGOs, scientists
○ Use prospective research designs, collect baseline data, and broaden the definition of *exposure* (e.g., include more social scientists on boards responsible for distributing research funds).	Federal government, scientists
○ Facilitate data sharing and access (e.g., coordinate research groups to avoid participant fatigue).	Federal government, private sector, scientists

NOTE: NGO = nongovernment organization.

Coastal communities surrounding the Gulf of Mexico continue to prove their resilience to catastrophic events, such as large oil spills, but need support adapting to changing conditions to manage disaster risk. To address risk effectively, communities will need support from government at all levels, nongovernment organizations, and industry. Using our synthesis of research on the mental health, economic, and community distress associated with the DWH oil spill and discussion of the synthesis with subject-matter experts, the recommendations provided in this report are intended to improve policy, practice, and research aimed at building resilience in Gulf Coast communities. The findings and recommendations presented here can be generalized to other large events that can cause a heavy human toll, such as hurricanes, flooding, and epidemics. Although research and practice need to address the nuances of specific events and community characteristics, the key messages in this report underscore best practices for disaster management that are broadly applicable.

Acknowledgments

We gratefully acknowledge the support of the Gulf of Mexico Research Initiative, members and partners of the Consortium for Resilient Gulf Communities, research participants, government agencies, nonprofit organizations, local communities that welcomed us into discussions, and community members who provided thoughtful comments and insights in response to our research questions and in drafts of this report. We are also grateful for comments provided by two reviewers: Baruch Fischhoff of Carnegie Mellon University and Jaime Madrigano of the RAND Corporation.

Abbreviations

CRGC	Consortium for Resilient Gulf Communities
DWH	Deepwater Horizon
GoMRI	Gulf of Mexico Research Initiative
GRHOP	Gulf Region Health Outreach Program
STRONG	Survey of Trauma, Resilience, and Opportunity in Neighborhoods in the Gulf
VoO	Vessels of Opportunity
WaTCH	Women and Their Children's Health

1. Introduction

Disasters like the 2010 Deepwater Horizon (DWH) oil spill should serve as turning points, after which society evaluates how to improve community efforts to prepare for, respond to, recover from, and prevent such catastrophes. Ten years after the DWH oil spill, it is time to assess the recommendations that have emerged from research on the mental health, economic, and community distress associated with this disaster. Local communities, government agencies, nonprofit organizations, and others are eager to know how best to mitigate risks. What have researchers learned about the impacts of the DWH oil spill on mental health, economic, and social functioning in communities surrounding the Gulf of Mexico? What do the research findings imply for effectively building community resilience in advance of another major oil spill?

The DWH oil spill was the largest in U.S. history, releasing an estimated 4.9 million barrels of oil into the Gulf of Mexico and affecting communities throughout the coastal Gulf of Mexico region.[1] The scale of the disaster motivated diverse stakeholders to examine human dimensions of the impacts and how communities' resilience to similar future threats could be improved. Moreover, ongoing dependence on oil and gas means that coastal regions remain at risk for future spills. This report seeks to address the following question: What could communities, government officials, nongovernmental organizations, businesses, and scientists do to build community resilience to future oil spills?

In addition to paying more than $20.8 billion in environmental damages, BP allocated $500 million for independent research on the oil spill's impacts.[2] This funding established the Gulf of Mexico Research Initiative (GoMRI). Over ten years, GoMRI distributed the funds for research activities aimed at improving society's ability to understand, respond to, and mitigate the impacts of petroleum pollution and associated stressors on the environment and public health in the region. About 4.2 percent of the GoMRI funding awarded through the competitive grant process (approximately $16.8 million of $400 million) was allocated to scientific studies of behavioral and socioeconomic impacts, population health, environmental risk assessment, and community capacity considerations (theme 5).[3] Additional studies have been supported by other programs, such as the National Academies of Sciences, Engineering and Medicine's Gulf Research Program and the National Institute of Environmental Health Sciences. However, there has been no comprehensive synthesis of studies on the mental health, economic, and community distress

---

[1] U.S. Coast Guard and National Response Team, 2011; National Commission on the BP Deepwater Horizon Oil Spill and Offshore Drilling, 2011.

[2] National Oceanic and Atmospheric Association, 2017.

[3] Personal communication with GoMRI officials.

associated with the DWH disaster on Gulf Coast communities. Furthermore, implications of those findings have yet to be distilled into recommendations for specific stakeholder groups.

Report Goal and Aims

In this report, researchers synthesize existing research to determine the opportunities and challenges facing stakeholders in the Gulf of Mexico as they attempt to build community resilience in advance of another large oil spill. We aim to

- identify key findings from research on the human dimensions of the DWH oil spill, particularly related to mental health, economic, and community distress
- provide recommendations, based on extant research, for improving Gulf Coast communities' ability to deal with the risks of a large oil spill.

We seek to provide guidance for the array of stakeholders that shape disaster resilience in coastal communities in the Gulf of Mexico region, particularly through policy, practice, and research activities. This initial synthesis focuses on lessons about DWH-related impacts from the social science research to date. We anticipate new and more-nuanced findings emerging in the future from ongoing research efforts, and these should be integrated into updated syntheses.

Study Approach

To address the report's objectives, the GoMRI-funded Consortium for Resilient Gulf Communities (CRGC) identified and reviewed 98 peer-reviewed articles and other reports on the DWH oil spill, which were published from 2010 through 2019 in the Web of Science and PubMed databases, as well as in several disaster-related databases (see Appendix A for detailed methods). The literature reflects diverse social science fields, topics, methods, populations, periods, and geographies. The diversity of studies prevents a formal meta-analysis, but we consider the disparate evidence across multiple studies to glean insights specific to each topic area (mental health, economic, and community distress) and to community resilience more broadly. Given the already diverse body of work related to DWH, we did not systematically examine studies on other oil spills (although some studies did compare DWH with the Exxon Valdez event).[4] We indicate where study effects are reported as statistically significant, but we also highlight the practical importance of providing a narrative summary for interpreting results across the larger body of work. In addition, although physical and mental health are closely related within the disaster context, our literature review for this report did not include studies that primarily examined physical health impacts. Other reports synthesizing research on physical

---

[4] Gill, Picou, and Ritchie, 2012; Gill et al., 2014.

health impacts are available elsewhere; the narrower focus of this report reflects the authors' expertise and the specific objectives of the funding allocated.[5]

Our review identified key findings and recommendations on three main human systems affected by the DWH oil spill: mental health, economic, and community functioning. Initial results of the literature review were presented to representatives of nongovernment organizations, academic researchers, and community leaders who attended a workshop in New Orleans on February 8, 2019. The workshop was designed to elicit feedback on the initial results and to identify recommendations for addressing community distress associated with large oil spills in the future. Details of relevant empirical papers are summarized in Appendix B, and the key messages presented at the workshop are provided in Appendix C.

Contextual Background

The DWH oil rig, leased by BP, exploded on April 20, 2010, about 50 miles offshore of southeast Louisiana. The explosion killed 11 men working on the rig; over almost three months, nearly 5 million barrels of crude oil spilled into the Gulf of Mexico from an ocean depth of around 5,000 feet—the largest marine oil spill in history.[6] More than 950 miles of the northern Gulf Coast, from eastern Texas to the Florida Panhandle, was affected by the oil.[7] The top panel of Figure 1.1 shows the maximum oiling along the coastline during 2010–2012; the bottom two panels show the amount of oiling in May 2011 and 2012, respectively. When the DWH oil spill occurred, the region had recently experienced severe hurricanes and flooding, and was still in the process of recovering from other catastrophic events, such as the 2005 Hurricanes Katrina and Rita.

---

[5] Aguilera et al., 2010; Eklund et al., 2019; Laffon, Pásaro, and Valdiglesias, 2016.

[6] National Commission on the BP Deepwater Horizon Oil Spill and Offshore Drilling, 2011.

[7] National Wildlife Federation, undated; Avery, 2010.

Figure 1.1. Maps of Shoreline Oiling at Maximum Oiling Conditions, One Year (May 2011), and Two Years (May 2012) After the Spill

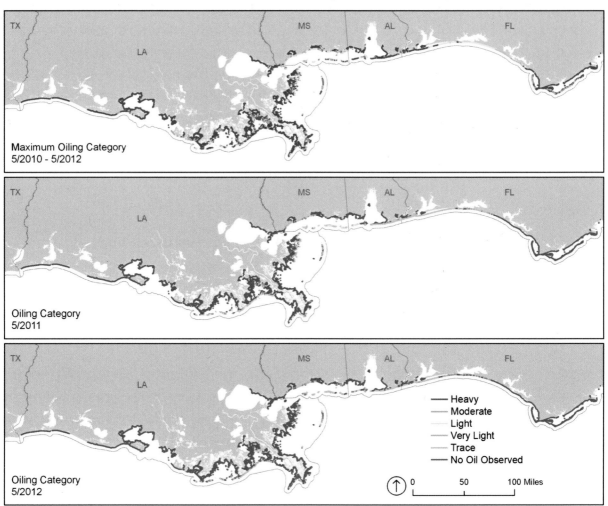

SOURCE: Michel et al., 2013.

The Gulf of Mexico is home to several major estuaries and supports commercial and recreational fishing, seafood processing, and tourism. Short-term fishing and drilling moratoriums were enacted immediately following the DWH oil spill. In the years after the oil spill, fishers faced threats from environmental contamination and stigma from consumer concerns about Gulf seafood safety.[8] The region's population is diverse, ranging from people whose ancestors have lived there for hundreds of years to very recent immigrants. The coastal region includes large cities like New Orleans, small towns, and rural areas. The fishing and oil production industries play a dominant role in the livelihoods of residents.

The DWH oil spill resulted in various claims, settlement, and litigation processes to address ecological, economic, health, and sociocultural damages in the region. Acting as the responsible

---

[8] Simon-Friedt et al., 2016; Singleton et al., 2016.

party for the disaster, BP set aside $20 billion to compensate affected parties for their economic losses.[9] From those funds, about $12 billion was paid to individuals, companies, and local governments for losses caused by damages to the Gulf's ecosystem. The compensation system implemented by BP was one of the largest in U.S. history, but the company was not prepared to handle the initial wave of almost 144,000 claims.[10] Subsequently, the Gulf Coast Claims facility was established, and it disbursed $6.3 billion to almost 225,000 claimants. In addition, the U.S. Department of Justice filed criminal and civil suits against three corporate defendants (BP, Transocean, and Halliburton). In 2013, the largest criminal resolution in U.S. history occurred when the Justice Department and BP settled the criminal case for $4 billion in penalties.[11] In December 2012, the Economic and Property Damages Settlement Agreement was approved, and in January 2013, the Medical Benefits Class Action Settlement Agreement was approved.

Overview of This Report

We first present a conceptual framework for organizing and understanding aspects of community resilience that are relevant to the DWH oil spill (Chapter 2). We then briefly summarize the key findings from a review of research literature (Chapters 3 through 5) and provide recommendations (Chapter 6) based on feedback from workshop participants. Overall conclusions are presented in Chapter 7. This report will be informative for members of government agencies responsible for disaster preparedness, response, and recovery; nongovernmental organizations working to improve community resilience; local community leaders working directly with coastal residents whose livelihoods depend on natural resources; private-sector companies involved in reducing risk; and scientists and donors (federal and private) responsible for distributing resources that support research in this field.

---

[9] Flocks and Davies, 2014.

[10] Avery, 2010.

[11] U.S. Environmental Protection Agency, 2013.

2. Conceptual Framework of Community Resilience and Vulnerability to Environmental Disasters

Community resilience is the sustained ability of a community to respond to, withstand, and recover from disaster events, such as large oil spills.[1] Place-based conceptualizations of social vulnerability emphasize that some people and communities suffer more than others after a disaster.[2] Over several decades, empirical research has clearly shown that disasters are complex social processes that play out over long periods of time and that multiple factors influence community resilience and vulnerability.[3] Using existing models of disaster risk, vulnerability, and resilience, we developed a conceptual framework (see Figure 2.1) to organize the findings and recommendations described in this report.[4] This figure is not a model for empirical testing; instead, it highlights the role of disasters as shocks impacting the nested set of individuals, communities, policies, and natural and built environments. A combination of community capacities and chronic stressors (working independently or through interaction) strongly influences the recovery (or dysfunction) trajectories of individuals and communities over time.

---

[1] Patel et al., 2017.

[2] Lee and Blanchard, 2012; Cutter et al., 2008; Oliver-Smith, 1996; Cutter, 1996; Cutter, Boruff, and Shirley, 2003; Quarantelli, 2005; Tierney, 2006.

[3] Gill and Picou, 1998; Cope et al., 2013; Quarantelli, 1989; Perry and Quarantelli, 2005.

[4] Cutter et al., 2008; Cutter, 1996; Chandra et al., 2011; Chandra et al., 2018; Picou, Marshall, and Gill, 2004; Hobfoll, 1989; Hobfoll, 1988; Norris et al., 2008; Wisner et al., 2004; Carney, 1998.

Figure 2.1. Conceptual Framework of Community Resilience and Vulnerability to Environmental Disasters

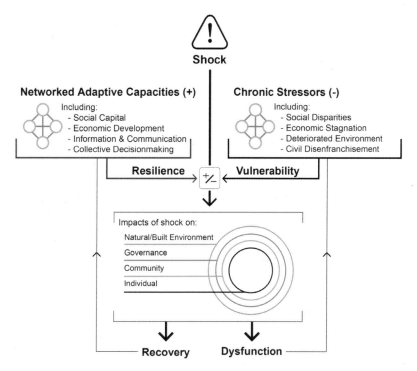

A key theme from prior research is that environmental contamination, such as an oil spill disaster, results in collective and individual stress for all communities.[5] How people weather and adapt to repeated exposure to stress depends on an array of psychological, sociodemographic, economic, physical, and other variables. Disaster impacts might be amplified by such chronic stressors as social disparities, economic stagnation, already deteriorated environments, and civil disenfranchisement. These stressors reflect *community allostatic load*, otherwise known as the "wear and tear" of repeated exposure to adversity.[6] Because Gulf Coast communities are heavily reliant on the oil and gas, fishing, and tourism industries, main sources of stress were resource loss, threat of resource loss, and failure to gain resources following investment.[7] Accordingly, such communities as fishers, which have high levels of economic, social, and cultural attachment to threatened, damaged, and depleted resources, are particularly vulnerable to increased stress because of the risk to their livelihoods.

Shock impacts may be buffered by *adaptive capacities*. Adaptive capacities can be grouped into four major categories.[8] *Economic development* is the volume, diversity, and distribution of economic resources in a community (i.e., those with more economic resources, a more diverse

---

[5] Hallman and Wandersman, 1992.

[6] Chandra et al., 2018.

[7] Hobfoll, 1989; Hobfoll, 1988.

[8] Norris et al., 2008.

economic base, and a more equitable distribution of economic resources will be more resilient). *Social capital* is the existence of social support, social network embeddedness, organizational linkages, and community attachment (i.e., those with higher levels of social support, greater network embeddedness, more linkages between organizations, and greater community attachment will be more resilient). *Information and communication* refers to accurate and timely information being available from trusted sources during a disaster. Finally, *collective decisionmaking* is the ability of community members to engage collaboratively to make decisions and act according to the outcome of those decisions.

The result of a shock is usually a mix of recovery and dysfunction—for example, a community's economy might recover quickly, but its members might continue to struggle with long-term mental health challenges. This combination of recovery and dysfunction influences adaptive capacities and stressors and creates the context for response to future stressful events. Stressful events originating from outside the community also influence the relationships between factors inside the community, making some stronger and others weaker than they otherwise would be. For example, people usually depend on their family and friends to support their well-being, but when disaster strikes, those relationships may become especially important, even if only temporarily. We use feedback loops to capture this dynamic and to show how recovery and dysfunction can feed into community capacities and chronic stressors.

3. Mental Health Distress Associated with the Deepwater Horizon Oil Spill

Key Findings

Evidence for mental health distress associated with the DWH oil spill is mixed, with a lack of baseline data and prospective studies limiting the potential conclusions that can be made about causal linkages between the oil spill and mental health symptoms. Researchers usually study people's mental health only after disaster strikes. However, to really understand which impacts were caused by the disaster, researchers must know how people were doing before the spill and monitor them over time to rule out competing explanations. Other methodological limitations arise from the practical challenge of collecting data in a disaster context, where comprehensive measures of diverse factors are simply not appropriate.

The findings reported, however, are still informative. Interestingly, even years after the spill, Gulf Coast residents report experiencing mental health distress that they associate with DWH, with the nature and strength of the reports differing across social groups. Studies used diverse research designs (cross-sectional and longitudinal), sampling strategies (from small purposive samples to very large population-based samples), sample types (clinical and nonclinical participants), and geographic areas (specific to one or a few Gulf States and regionwide). The key findings reported in these studies are summarized in Table 3.1; more details are provided in the following sections of this chapter.

Table 3.1. Key Findings from Research on Mental Health

Overall impacts	Diverse studies provide mixed evidence for short- and long-term mental health distress (depression, anxiety, and posttraumatic stress) associated with the DWH oil spill.
Chronic stressors	Life disruption (particularly income loss), prior trauma, and various sociodemographic characteristics are important drivers of negative mental health symptoms.
Adaptive capacities	Higher levels of social capital—particularly social support, sense of community, and perceived resiliency—have a protective impact against spill-related stress in most cases, except for groups with high attachment to damaged resources (e.g., fishing households).
Varying recovery and dysfunction	Some social groups reported experiencing more distress than others, in part because of differing levels and types of prior trauma, disruption from the oil spill, or available support.

Extent and Nature of Mental Health Distress Associated with the Deepwater Horizon Oil Spill

Assessments of the mental health of Gulf Coast communities have demonstrated mixed findings regarding psychological disruption following the DWH oil spill. Results across a range of sample sizes and types, locations, and time frames suggest that the oil spill was associated with increased reports of symptoms consistent with depression,[1] anxiety,[2] and posttraumatic stress.[3] However, two large, population-based surveys (conducted by the Substance Abuse and Mental Health Services Administration and Centers for Disease Control and Prevention) in the Gulf Coast region suggested only modest or minimal changes in behavioral health before versus after the oil spill at the aggregate level.[4] As is typical of most disaster studies, planned pre-post designs were impossible, so causal mechanisms cannot be examined in these studies. In short, although important information was obtained about patterns of mental health symptoms in the months and years after the oil spill, none of the studies were prospective, and the findings might have multiple alternative plausible explanations (e.g., the comparison and exposed samples are different; other experiences may have affected the mental health of participants in the two groups).

In the months immediately after the spill, a Community Assessment for Public Health Emergency Response (CASPER) of residents in coastal Alabama and Mississippi found that about 15–24 percent of respondents reported depressive symptoms and 21–35 percent reported symptoms consistent with an anxiety disorder.[5] Overall, the CASPER respondents reported a higher proportion of negative quality-of-life indicators and social context outcomes compared with estimates from recent Behavioral Risk Factor Surveillance System (BRFSS) surveys (national telephone surveys conducted by the Centers for Disease Control and Prevention). In 2011, about 9–15 percent of respondents reported depressive symptoms and about 13–20 percent reported symptoms consistent with anxiety—these proportions were still higher than those in the BRFSS surveys, but lower than those in the 2010 CASPERs.[6] The Gulf State Population Survey

---

[1] Buttke, Vagi, Bayleyegn, et al., 2012; Buttke, Vagi, Schnall, et al., 2012; Cherry et al., 2015; Drescher, Schulenberg, and Smith, 2014; Fan et al., 2015; Grattan et al., 2011; Morris et al., 2013; Osofsky, Hansel, et al., 2015; Rung et al., 2016; Ramchand et al., 2019; Kwok, Mcgrath, et al., 2017; Gaston et al., 2017.

[2] Buttke, Vagi, Bayleyegn, et al., 2012; Buttke, Vagi, Schnall, et al., 2012; Cherry et al., 2015; Drescher, Schulenberg, and Smith, 2014; Grattan et al., 2011; Morris et al., 2013; Ramchand et al., 2019; Kwok, McGrath, et al., 2017.

[3] Gill, Picou, and Ritchie, 2012; Gill et al., 2014; Cherry et al., 2015; Drescher, Schulenberg, and Smith, 2014; Kwok, McGrath, et al., 2017; Aiena et al., 2016; Osofsky, Hansel, et al., 2015; Osofsky, Osofsky, and Hansel, 2011.

[4] Gould et al., 2015.

[5] Buttke, Vagi, Bayleyegn, et al., 2012.

[6] Buttke, Vagi, Schnall, et al., 2012.

found similar levels of mental health symptoms reported in a representative survey of 38,361 residents conducted from 2010 to 2011 in four Gulf States.[7]

Subsequent studies reported psychological distress several years after the DHW oil spill, but evidence for an association between the distress and the oil spill is mixed and, as above, baseline data are lacking, so a causal explanation cannot be determined. The Women and Their Children's Health (WaTCH) study[8]—a telephone survey conducted from 2012 to 2014 with a population-based sample of 2,842 women living in southern coastal Louisiana—found that more than 28 percent of the sample reported symptoms of depression. The WaTCH study also found that 13 percent of the sample reported severe mental distress, 16 percent reported an increase in the number of partner fights, and 11 percent reported an increase in the intensity of partner fights. How the rates of symptoms in the WaTCH sample compare with rates in this population of women (i.e., those with children living in the Gulf region) is unknown. In 2016, the Survey of Trauma, Resilience, and Opportunity in Neighborhoods in the Gulf (STRONG) provided prevalence estimates for various mental and behavioral outcomes from a population-representative sample of 2,520 coastal residents in Texas, Louisiana, Alabama, Mississippi, and Florida.[9] Even six years after the DWH oil spill, that study reported that resource loss attributed to the oil spill was statistically significantly associated with positive screens for depression and anxiety. Around 16 percent of residents screened positive for depression, 20 percent for anxiety, and 27 percent for alcohol misuse; less than 20 percent reported access to mental health care. Mental and behavioral health outcomes for specific groups within the sample are presented in Table 3.2. The reference category is the category with which the other categories are compared. For instance, compared with Texas as the reference category, the percentage of respondents screening positive for depression is statistically significantly higher in Mississippi.

Table 3.2. Mental and Behavioral Health Among Residents in the Gulf Coast Region

	Depression Screen (% SE)	Anxiety Screen (% SE)	Alcohol Misuse Screen (% SE)
Total	16.2 (1.5)	19.9 (1.6)	27.3 (1.7)
Louisiana	18.1 (2.4)	25.2 (3.0)	35.9 (3.4)[a]
Texas (reference)	12.0 (2.1)	16.5 (2.6)	26.8 (3.2)
Mississippi	20.3 (2.9)[a]	24.1 (3.3)	24.7 (3.0)
Alabama	13.4 (2.4)	20.2 (2.9)	24.9 (3.0)
Florida	19.4 (2.9)[a]	22.5 (3.1)	26.5 (3.1)
Sex			

[7] Fan et al., 2015.

[8] Rung et al., 2016.

[9] Ramchand et al., 2019.

	Depression Screen (% SE)	Anxiety Screen (% SE)	Alcohol Misuse Screen (% SE)
Male (reference)	17.3 (2.3)	15.6 (2.2)	31.9 (2.7)
Female	15.2 (1.9)	24.0 (2.4)[a]	22.8 (2.1)[a]
Age			
18–34	14.3 (2.9)	19.3 (3.3)	33.2 (3.9)
35–64 (reference)	18.6 (2.3)	23.3 (2.4)	26.7 (2.4)
65+	13.3 (2.3)	12.9 (2.2)[a]	20.5 (2.4)
Race/ethnicity			
Hispanic	14.8 (3.5)	22.1 (4.3)	27.2 (4.4)
White (reference)	16.5 (2.0)	18.8 (2.0)	30.0 (2.2)
Black	18.2 (3.0)	23.5 (3.9)	19.0 (3.6)[a]
Other	12.6 (7.0)	12.7 (7.0)	22.1 (9.2)
Sexual identity			
LGB (lesbian, gay, and bisexual)	19.6 (8.4)	27.5 (9.0)	37.6 (9.0)
Non-LGB (reference)	16.1 (1.5)	19.7 (1.7)	27.4 (1.8)
Industry at the time of the DWH oil spill[b]			
Oil and gas	12.9 (2.7)	18.3 (3.4)	34.6 (4.5)
Fishing or seafood	23.1 (4.7)[a]	19.8 (3.8)	28.5 (6.1)
Tourism	17.5 (4.0)	19.7 (4.4)	27.5 (4.8)
In region at the time of the DWH oil spill			
No (reference)	24.3 (5.2)	30.7 (5.3)	23.8 (4.5)
Yes	14.9 (1.5)[a]	18.1 (1.6)[a]	27.8 (1.9)

SOURCE: Ramchand et al., 2019, p. 893.
NOTE: SE = standard error.
[a] Statistically significant difference with reference category, indicated by 95-percent confidence intervals that do not contain the null value (1.00).
[b] Reference for industry at the time of the DWH oil spill is not participating in any of the industries.

Predictors of Mental Health Distress

Both direct and indirect exposure to the DWH disaster seem to drive reports of negative mental health symptoms.[10] Broadly, people reporting greater disruption in their lives, work, family, and social engagements were found to have worse mental health.[11] For instance, a study of a sample of adult clients in mental health agencies in coastal Mississippi in 2011 found higher levels of psychological distress (depression, anxiety, stress, and posttraumatic stress disorder) among adults reporting that the DWH spill affected their finances, social relationships, or

---

[10] Gill, Picou, and Ritchie, 2012; Gill et al., 2014; Fan et al., 2015.

[11] Gill, Picou, and Ritchie, 2012; Gill et al., 2014; Osofsky, Osofsky, and Hansel, 2011.

physical health.[12] A study with a purposive sample from coastal communities in Alabama suggested that suicide proneness was more likely among residents who lacked resources, experienced distress, and coped by avoidance.[13] Other literature points to the emotional stress related to the oil spill as a possible cause of increased physical health risk (e.g., heart attacks).[14] Some studies suggest that the strongest predictor of anxiety and depression was reported income loss related to the oil spill.[15] A study of residents in coastal Alabama and Florida found that, compared with people with stable incomes, people reporting spill-related income loss had statistically significantly worse scores on anxiety, depression, and other behavioral health measures. They also were less resilient and more likely to use behavioral disengagement as a coping strategy.[16]

In several studies, prior trauma has been identified as an important predictor for behavioral health problems associated with DWH.[17] For instance, prior exposure to loss from hurricanes, such as Hurricane Katrina, predicted increased symptoms of oil spill distress.[18] Another recent study found that individuals with more-traumatic experiences (such as being in a bad car accident) in their history had a statistically significant higher risk for behavioral health problems (e.g., depression, anxiety, alcohol use) after controlling for demographic factors and DWH exposure.[19] After controlling for other trauma in this study, there was no evidence of an association between mental health problems and DWH exposure.[20]

Negative mental health impacts associated with the DHW oil spill were related to other characteristics of individuals and communities. Particularly vulnerable groups included children,[21] women,[22] people with less wealth,[23] people who were unemployed or with lower income,[24] and minorities.[25] Other vulnerable groups included people with lower self-perceived

---

[12] Drescher, Schulenberg, and Smith, 2014.

[13] Bell, Langhinrichsen-Rohling, and Selwyn, 2020.

[14] Strelitz et al., 2018.

[15] Morris et al., 2013; Rung et al., 2016.

[16] Grattan et al., 2011.

[17] Osofsky, Osofsky, and Hansel, 2011; Sandifer et al., 2017; Sandifer and Walker, 2018; Goldmann and Galea, 2014; Neria, Nandi, and Galea, 2008; Osofsky, Osofsky, Weems, et al., 2014; Hansel et al., 2015; King et al., 2015; Ayer et al., 2019; Rung et al., 2015.

[18] Cherry et al., 2015; Osofsky, Hansel, et al., 2015; Osofsky, Osofsky, and Hansel, 2011.

[19] Ayer et al., 2019.

[20] Ayer et al., 2019.

[21] Fan et al., 2015; Gould et al., 2015; Hansel et al., 2015; King et al., 2015.

[22] Cope et al., 2013; Fan et al., 2015; Rung et al., 2016; Ramchand et al., 2019; Harville et al., 2018.

[23] Cope et al., 2013; Cherry et al., 2015; Hansel et al., 2015.

[24] Cope et al., 2013.

[25] Cope et al., 2013; Patel et al., 2018; Ngo et al., 2014; Austin et al., 2014.

resiliency and lower perceived meaning in life;[26] people with low religiosity living in highly religious areas;[27] and lower levels of social capital, including social support and sense of community.[28] One study suggested that once social support and cognitive social capital (shared understanding) were accounted for, disaster-related economic exposure is no longer associated with such mental health outcomes as depression.[29] Another study highlighted commercial fishers as particularly at risk for depression symptoms, consistent with the stress of losing multiple types of resources (e.g., job security, social networks, money, boat, self-esteem); these detrimental impacts were not related only to the DWH oil spill, but also the 2005 hurricane season.[30] Structural equation analyses of survey data from coastal Mississippi survivors of 2005's Hurricane Katrina and the 2010 DWH oil spill showed an indirect relationship between *posttraumatic growth* (positive changes during or after adversity that lead to better psychological well-being) and depressive symptoms through loneliness; social capital was directly related to posttraumatic growth but related to loneliness only indirectly through posttraumatic growth.[31]

Analyses of data from a large population-based study—the National Institute of Environmental Health Sciences Gulf Long-Term Follow-Up Study—suggest that oil spill response and clean-up workers with high amounts of total hydrocarbon exposure or potentially stressful jobs following the DWH oil spill had an increased prevalence of depression and posttraumatic stress.[32] Other analyses suggest that physical health symptoms contribute to clean-up workers' risk for mental health symptoms (posttraumatic stress, major depression, and generalized anxiety disorder) but that longer duration of clean-up work and higher work-related oil exposure were associated with higher household income, which in turn was associated with lower anxiety and depression.[33] Of the clean-up workers who reported accessing mental health services, 8.2 percent reported using counseling and 9.2 percent reported using medication.[34]

The above studies highlight a critical finding—that there is the potential for different experiences across social groups in environmental disaster contexts, likely because there are complex relationships between individual and community characteristics and their impacts on mental health. For instance, analyses of the STRONG data showed an inverse relationship between social support and positive screens for depression for most Gulf Coast residents, but among those with ties to the fishing industry, greater social support was associated with a higher

---

[26] Aiena et al., 2016; Osofsky, Osofsky, et al., 2015; Shenesey and Langhinichsen-Rohling, 2015.

[27] Cherry et al., 2015.

[28] Cope et al., 2013; Cherry et al., 2015; Rung et al., 2015; Rung et al., 2017; Cherry et al., 2016.

[29] Rung et al., 2017.

[30] Cherry et al., 2015.

[31] Lee et al., 2019.

[32] Kwok, McGrath, et al., 2017.

[33] Lowe et al., 2016.

[34] Lowe et al., 2015.

probability of screening positive for depression.[35] In another report based on analyses of the STRONG data, researchers found that living in a highly religious area might magnify behavioral health problems, such as problem drinking, among disaster-affected individuals for whom religion is not very salient.[36] In this case, we speculate that the distribution of social resources was uneven across religious and nonreligious individuals. These studies hint at important mechanisms that could contribute to the vulnerability of some individuals, but further empirical research is needed to quantify impacts and the role of specific factors in determining outcomes.

Limitations

Several methodological challenges limit the conclusions that can be drawn from the findings reported above. First, as is typical of most research on the human dimensions of disasters, the above-cited research is limited in its ability to identify causal relationships. In particular, longitudinal designs are rare and predisaster baseline data are lacking. There is also limited access to important contextual variables. Such limitations derive, in large part, from the reactive approach, which collects data only after a disaster happens, rather than using baseline data and prospective designs.[37] Second, to reduce demands on (already stressed) survey participants, to meet slim research budgets, or to collect data in a timely manner, assessments of mental health symptoms or disaster-related stressors typically are not comprehensive.[38] Instead, researchers tend to rely on short-form or screener assessments. Third, different studies use different sampling and measurement strategies.[39] For instance, depression or anxiety may be measured with a two-item screening instrument or a longer, more-comprehensive set of items on a questionnaire. In addition, studies often fail to include people who leave a disaster-affected region (e.g., to find employment elsewhere), making it hard to capture the full impact of an event. Different measurement and sampling approaches often reflect different research questions, but also might reflect the distributed, and often disconnected, efforts of diverse research teams. Research societies and funders could encourage coordination among efforts (without artificially enforcing rigid standards), potentially resulting in greater comparability across studies. Finally, previous research suggests a close relationship between mental and physical health in a disaster context, but our review excluded studies that primarily examined physical health impacts associated with the DWH oil spill. Other reports synthesizing research on physical health impacts are available.[40]

---

[35] Parks et al., 2019.

[36] Drakeford et al., 2019.

[37] Parker et al., 2019.

[38] Osofsky, Palinkas, and Galloway, 2010.

[39] Galea, Maxwell, and Norris, 2008.

[40] Aguilera et al., 2010; Kwok, Engel, et al., 2017; Eklund et al., 2019; Laffon, Pásaro, and Valdiglesias, 2016.

4. Economic Impacts Associated with the Deepwater Horizon Oil Spill

Key Findings

Local fishing, oil and gas, and tourism industries experienced substantial damages in the short term, but economic impacts differed across the Gulf Coast region. In the long term, high proportions of households reported negative financial experiences associated with the oil spill. The nature of the economic impacts of the DWH oil spill have been documented in about ten papers and reports over the past ten years. Identifying causal effects from these studies is difficult, however, because multiple economic or other changes may have occurred at the same time. In addition, aggregate analyses rely on assumptions about the capacity of individuals and communities to respond to shocks, potentially under- or overrepresenting resilience in the region. Key findings are summarized in Table 4.1, and relevant studies are described in more detail in the rest of this chapter.

Table 4.1. Key Findings from Research on Economic Impacts

Overall impacts	Economic losses from the DHW oil spill to the commercial fishing, oil and gas, and tourism industries were limited to the short term. Years after the oil spill, however, high proportions of households report very negative impacts on their financial situations.
Chronic stressors	The most-severe economic impacts were reported by poorer households.
Adaptive capacities	Aggregate analyses by industry showed that unemployment rates were not permanently affected by the spill.
Varying recovery and dysfunction	Economic impacts were highly heterogenous, with a net increase in employment and wages in some areas (e.g., in Louisiana, partly because of the work needed for spill clean-up) but a decline in employment and wages in other areas (e.g., Florida).

Extent and Nature of Economic Impacts Associated with the Deepwater Horizon Oil Spill

Economic impacts of the DWH oil spill were broad and substantial, at least in the relatively short term. In addition to the damage associated with onshore oiling, there were economic consequences of the response and recovery, including the temporary ban on fishing and damages to the region's reputation as a fishing and tourism destination.[1]

---

[1] Nadeau et al., 2014; Larkin, Huffaker, and Clouser, 2013.

Although there is debate about the exact level of economic losses, studies suggest that the DWH oil spill resulted in substantial damages to commercial fishing,[2] the oil and gas industry,[3] and tourism.[4] For instance, recreation losses alone amounted to between $585 and $661 million,[5] depending on the number of factors included in the analysis. These amounts are similar to the total recovery costs and economic and environmental losses associated with Spain's 2002 Prestige oil spill.[6] Immediately after the DWH oil spill, fishery closures and consumer-related seafood safety concerns caused considerable economic harm to the region.[7] One study conducted soon after the oil spill predicted that the spill could result in $3.7 billion in revenue losses and 22,000 lost jobs in commercial fisheries, recreational fisheries, and mariculture over a seven-year period.[8] In contrast to the predictive approach, more-recent analysis, based on observed data of Gulf blue crab fishing and analyzed using a quasiexperimental difference-in-differences approach, suggested that there were substantial declines in crab landings in 2010 (see Figures 4.1 and 4.2). The analyses showed that declines were driven largely by the reduction in crabbing trips. Both trips and landings largely recovered (with no statistically significant differences between observed and counterfactual counties or parishes affected by the spill) by 2011.[9]

---

[2] Carroll et al., 2016.

[3] U.S. Department of Commerce, 2010.

[4] Nadeau et al., 2014; Alvarez et al., 2014; English et al., 2018; Glasgow and Train, 2018; Whitehead et al., 2018.

[5] Alvarez et al., 2014; English et al., 2018.

[6] Loureiro et al., 2006.

[7] Upton, 2011.

[8] Sumaila et al., 2012.

[9] Fiore, Bond, and Nataraj, 2020.

Figure 4.1. Gulf Blue Crab Landings

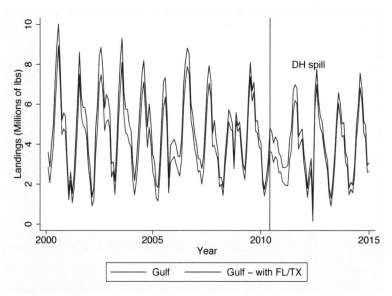

SOURCE: Fiore, Bond, and Nataraj, 2020, p. 23.
NOTE: This figure depicts monthly commercial blue crab landings in the Gulf States (Alabama, Louisiana, Mississippi, Texas, west coast of Florida) based on landings data downloaded from the National Oceanic and Atmospheric Association Commercial Landings database. DH = Deepwater Horizon.

Figure 4.2. Louisiana Blue Crab Landings

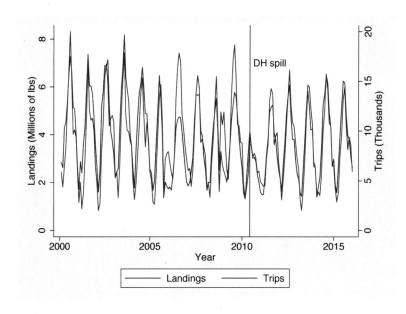

SOURCE: Fiore, Bond, and Nataraj, 2020, p. 24.
NOTE: This figure depicts annual commercial blue crab landings in Louisiana based on data provided by the Louisiana Department of Wildlife and Fisheries. DH = Deepwater Horizon.

Economic impacts were highly heterogenous.[10] By region, parishes in Louisiana with oil-intensive economies, as well as coastal counties in Alabama, experienced a net increase in overall employment and wages in 2010, likely because they received resources for cleaning up the spill. In contrast, Florida counties outside the Florida Panhandle reported a decline in employment, while coastal counties in Texas, Mississippi, and the Florida Panhandle did not exhibit any changes in overall employment.[11] Impacts of the oil spill also varied across and within industry, affecting fishing, tourism, and oil industries to different extents and in different ways.[12] For example, the overall impact of the oil spill on the fishing industry was negative, but the extent varied by subsector, with harvesting, dealing, processing, distributing, market, and restaurants each being affected in different magnitudes.[13]

Furthermore, economic impacts varied by layer of analysis; impacts on individuals and communities could differ from the impacts on the industries on which they relied.[14] For instance, even though many deep-water rigs in the Gulf of Mexico were not producing during the moratorium, drilling contractors, rig operators, and well servicing firms mostly retained their highly skilled employees, at least initially. Although oil production stopped, impacts on jobs related to drilling operations were limited.[15]

In striking contrast to the findings reported from aggregate, macroeconomic analyses, surveys at the individual or household level found that respondents self-reported notable economic impacts associated with the DWH oil spill. In the months after the spill, about 20 to 36 percent of coastal households in Louisiana, Mississippi, and Alabama reported that their income had decreased as a result of the oil spill, with about 8 percent of households reporting losing a job.[16] Poorer residents (those earning less than $25,000 in annual household income) were more likely to report having lost income than those earning more.[17] Initial income losses did not seem to be offset by cash or gift cards from BP. According to 2010's Coastal Population Impact Study, only about 5 percent of coastal residents reported receiving any cash or gift cards from BP, although more than 15 percent believed that they might have been eligible for compensation for health consequences of the spill.[18] Individuals who were able to offset initial acute economic

---

[10] Austin et al., 2014.

[11] Aldy, 2014.

[12] Nadeau et al., 2014; Carroll et al., 2016.

[13] Carroll et al., 2016.

[14] Nadeau et al., 2014; Carroll et al., 2016; Aldy, 2014.

[15] U.S. Department of Commerce, 2010.

[16] Buttke, Vagi, Bayleyegn, et al., 2012; Abramson et al., 2010.

[17] Abramson et al., 2010.

[18] Abramson et al., 2010.

losses by large-sum BP payments (e.g., for clean-up activities including BP's Vessels of Opportunity [VoO] program) likely experienced more-modest mental health impacts.[19]

Reports of negative economic impacts from surveys of households continued in subsequent years. In 2011, coastal Alabama residents reported experiencing "very negative" (33 percent) or "somewhat negative" (40 percent) economic impacts.[20] From 2012 to 2014, the WaTCH survey found that 38 percent of households reported experiencing a "negative or somewhat negative" impact on their financial situation; 25 percent reported that they lost income at a business because of the oil spill.[21] In a 2017 survey of three Gulf communities—Port Sulphur, Louisiana; Galliano, Louisiana; and Bayou La Batre, Alabama—more than 22 percent of respondents reported losing their job after the oil spill.[22]

Although economic losses are restricted to the short term at the macroeconomic scale of industry, this does not preclude long-term individual impacts for those in that industry or outside it. Indeed, there is no guarantee from the industry-scale secondary data that the individuals that composed the fishing industry in the pre-spill period are the same as those operating in the post-spill period.

Limitations

There are several methodological limitations associated with the studies cited here. First, it can be difficult to identify the causal impact of the oil spill on economic outcomes. Although both pre-spill and post-spill data exist for many economic indicators, including fisheries landings, employment, and wages, it is not clear that all changes observed between the pre-spill and post-spill periods were caused by the spill, as many other economic changes occurred at the same time. Some of the studies described above aim to address this challenge by identifying appropriate counterfactuals for economic outcomes in the Gulf—other areas that would have exhibited the same pattern as the Gulf in the absence of the spill.[23] However, it is possible that these counterfactuals were themselves affected by events in coastal Gulf areas or that they experienced other changes that affected their economic outcomes.

Second, some estimates of potential damages (e.g., Sumaila et al., 2012) were developed soon after the spill and relied on several assumptions about how the impacts of the spill would affect both biology and markets. These estimates typically rely on *ex ante* models (which are based on predictions of future outcomes) as opposed to *ex post* models (which are based on observed data after the event) and often involve restrictive assumptions about the capacity of

---

[19] Shultz et al., 2015.

[20] Gill et al., 2014.

[21] Peres et al., 2016.

[22] Patel et al., 2018.

[23] English et al., 2018; Whitehead et al., 2018.

individuals and communities to respond to shocks. This may underrepresent the resilience of the region because the ways in which consumers or industries change their behavior are not explicitly modeled. Alternatively, the economic analyses might have overrepresented the resilience of the region because the aggregate approach does not preclude long-term, micro-level, individual impacts for those within or outside an industry, such as fishing. As noted above, the individuals operating in the fishing industry might not be the same in the pre-spill and post-spill periods. Finally, the estimates of recreational damages from the spill are based on modeling individuals' choices of which sites to visit, which relies on a variety of assumptions about individuals' trade-offs between site amenities and travel costs.[24]

---

[24] Alvarez et al., 2014; English et al., 2018.

5. Community Distress Associated with the Deepwater Horizon Oil Spill

Key Findings

Studies suggest severe disruption to Gulf Coast residents in some social contexts, including increased hostilities and weakened networks associated with the DWH oil spill. Different experiences of loss and recovery were reported by different groups, with fishing households reporting the most disruption. Evidence for community distress comes from about 20 studies that include community-based participatory methods, random sampling, qualitative and quantitative analyses, and a focus on immediate and longer-term impacts in various coastal locations. A challenge in interpreting the findings relates to the many potential ways of defining *community*. In addition, the role of some community characteristics in adaptation processes might change over time, but the longitudinal data needed to assess trajectories typically are not available. Key findings from the research are summarized in Table 5.1, and more details about these studies are provided in the text below.

Table 5.1. Key Findings from Research on Community Distress

Overall impacts	Conditions following the DWH oil spill are consistent with an environment that would negatively impact community well-being by reducing trust in authorities, weakening social networks, increasing perceptions of inequitable distribution of post-spill resources, and increasing domestic violence.
Chronic stressors	Substantial portions of coastal households (e.g., nearly 38 percent of an Alabama sample) were involved directly or indirectly in some type of claims, settlement, or litigation activity associated with the DWH oil spill. Uncertainty over the extent of oil spill impacts, competing narratives of responsibility and blame, protracted litigation or compensation processes, and perceptions of injustice related to these factors are chronic stressors.
Adaptive capacities	Communities are variably positioned in terms of vulnerability (e.g., fishing dependence) and resilience (e.g., social capital and community attachment).
Varying recovery and dysfunction	Different groups demonstrate different experiences of loss and recovery. Fishing households in particular report high levels of DWH-related disruption of social routines.

Extent and Nature of Community Distress Associated with the Deepwater Horizon Oil Spill

Gulf Coast communities are often close-knit and well connected, which usually creates good sources of support in difficult times. However, community conditions associated with BP's management of the clean-up and compensation processes following the DWH oil spill were typical of an environment that is likely to increase social conflict and reduce social support.[1] The spill was associated with reports of an erosion of trust in authorities, disrupted social ties, perceived increased social inequities, and increased domestic violence. A 2013 telephone survey of 1,216 coastal Alabama residents found that almost 23 percent of the sample were personally involved with some type of claims, settlement, or litigation activity associated with the DWH oil spill.[2] In addition, nearly 16 percent indicated that someone else in their household was part of DWH-related settlement or legal activities. Nearly 65 percent of those surveyed indicated that the compensation issues had been as distressing as the oil spill itself. Analyses showed that being part of the compensation process was one of the strongest contributors to intrusive stress among coastal residents.

Research on the compensation process following the DWH oil spill suggests that the process for distributing claims was perceived by residents to be random and to lack transparency, resulting in negative social comparisons and competition.[3] Despite substantial and fairly prompt economic aid, compensation programs enacted by BP, the Gulf Coast Claims Facility, and then the Deepwater Horizon Economic Claims Center have been viewed as problematic because these organizations use different definitions of compensable loss and there is perceived subjectivity in the procedures.[4] Focus groups and interviews conducted 20 months after the spill revealed that the programs were associated with resentment among residents, who "began bickering and fighting about money" and consequently limited their social interactions.[5]

Similarly, BP's VoO program, which made about $594 million in payments to existing fishing and commercial crews to support clean-up activities,[6] was perceived as arbitrarily employing recreational boats rather than out-of-work fishing vessels.[7] Many fishermen were able to leverage their expertise to participate in VoO, but the program was not suitable for others, who did not have the necessary resources (e.g., an idle boat).[8] Environments in which residents become pitted against one another have been called *corrosive communities*.[9] This environment is more common following technological disasters, such as oil spills, than after disasters considered to be beyond human control (e.g., hurricanes), especially when response efforts by the responsible parties provoke confusion and frustration rather than alleviate suffering.

---

[1] Austin et al., 2014; Palinkas, 2012.

[2] Ritchie, Gill, and Long, 2018.

[3] Mayer, Running, and Bergstrand, 2015; Halmo, Griffith, and Stoffle, 2019; Barker, 2011.

[4] Flocks and Davies, 2014; Austin et al., 2014.

[5] Mayer, Running, and Bergstrand, 2015.

[6] Upton, 2011.

[7] Mayer, Running, and Bergstrand, 2015; Halmo, Griffith, and Stoffle, 2019.

[8] Aldy, 2014; Shultz et al., 2015.

[9] Gill and Picou, 1998; Picou, Marshall, and Gill, 2004, Freudenberg, 1993; Erikson, 1976.

An additional signal of community distress is indicated in evidence that the DWH oil spill was associated with an increase in reports of domestic violence.[10] In the WaTCH study, nearly 16 percent of the sample reported an increase in the number of fights with their partner since the oil spill and 11 percent reported an increase in the intensity of fights.[11] Likewise, among partners of clean-up workers, the prevalence of an increased number of partner fights was 33 percent, which was associated with both economic and physical exposure (after controlling for other correlated variables).[12] Analysis showed that the detrimental impact of economic exposure on mental health symptoms, such as depression, could be explained almost entirely by economic exposure's detrimental impact on social resources (e.g., counting on family or friends for everyday favors).[13]

The community distress related to the DWH oil spill has been experienced unevenly by different groups. In particular, those relying more heavily on natural resources to earn their livelihood have been shown to be more vulnerable.[14] Evidence from the Community Oil Spill Survey (COSS) suggests that households with ties to the oil-gas and fishing-seafood industries were statistically significantly more likely than others to blame BP and the federal government for the consequences of the disaster, and to be more distrustful of these entities. Analyses of four waves of the COSS (conducted from 2010 to 2013) show that the odds of blaming BP and the federal government for the DWH oil spill held relatively steady over time, while the odds of blaming the state government increased over time.[15] Importantly, individuals' assessments of the trustworthiness of various institutional actors are complex and depend on their social backgrounds, experiences with the oil spill, and trust in information sources.[16] Some respondents in the COSS samples continued to report that their pre-spill routines were disrupted three years after the DWH oil spill. Disruption of routine behaviors was more likely for individuals with ties to the fishing industry (both fishing alone and in combination with oil work) than for those employed in the oil industry, as shown in Figure 5.1.[17]

---

[10] Rung et al., 2016; Rung et al., 2015.

[11] Rung et al., 2016.

[12] Rung et al., 2015.

[13] Rung et al., 2017.

[14] Gill, Picou, and Ritchie, 2012; Gill et al., 2014; Cope et al., 2013; Cope et al., 2016; Safford, Ulrich-Schad, and Hamilton, 2012; Parks et al., 2018.

[15] Cope et al., 2016.

[16] Safford, Ulrich-Schad, and Hamilton, 2012; Lesen et al., 2019; Petrun Sayers et al., 2019.

[17] Parks et al., 2018.

Figure 5.1. Levels of Disruption of Routine by Employment over Time

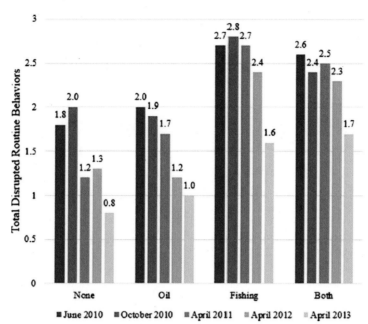

SOURCE: Parks et al., 2018.

A 2015 telephone survey of coastal residents in Alabama and Florida found that respondents who reported feeling angry or distressed by the oil spill had increased pro-environmental changes in their political behaviors, personal routines, and attitudes toward environmental issues generally and offshore oil drilling specifically.[18] One factor that may have helped some coastal communities relates to involvement in citizen science activities, which increased after the DWH oil spill.[19] Some authors suggest that citizen science enhances public health emergency preparedness by empowering communities to take collective action, improving system response capabilities, and generating relevant data to mitigate adverse health impacts.[20]

Limitations

Several methodological challenges limit the conclusions about community distress that can be drawn from the findings reported above. Perhaps the most fundamental challenge is deciding what is meant by *community*. Individuals and households can possess a sense of community through attachment to place, connections to others, and integration into local institutions. But communities are also places characterized by social and economic structures, physical infrastructure, and environmental conditions. Ultimately, these units of analysis are nested (i.e.,

---

[18] Bergstrand and Mayer, 2017.

[19] Chari, Blumenthal, and Matthews, 2019.

[20] McCormick, 2012; Sullivan et al., 2018.

individuals and households are nested within communities of place). Although some relevant measures can be captured with secondary data (e.g., basic population and economic characteristics), much can be accessed only by labor-intensive primary data collection (e.g., individual-level dispositions about community, livelihoods, and environment). Additionally, understanding adaptive capacity to social disruption requires tracking change over time. Doing so acknowledges that impacts and adaptation are about trajectories and process. As an illustration, research has shown that people with greater community attachment held more-negative emotions in the immediate aftermath of the DWH oil spill,[21] but they came to have more-positive emotions than others as time went on.[22] Furthermore, longitudinal data and pre-post disaster data are unusual, because they are costly, labor-intensive, and, by the very nature of disasters, difficult to collect.

---

[21] Lee and Blanchard, 2012.

[22] Cope et al., 2013.

6. Recommendations

In this chapter, we return to the following question: What could communities, government officials, nongovernmental organizations, businesses, and scientists do to build community resilience to future oil spills? Drawing on the findings from the research reviewed earlier and a much larger body of work on disaster risk, vulnerability, and resilience, we explore opportunities and challenges for different stakeholder groups. We describe five recommendations (summarized in Table 6.1) that surfaced as repeated themes in the literature reviewed and our workshop discussions. This section focuses primarily on what changes are needed in policy, practice, and research to help address the negative impacts of large oil spills on communities and to build community resilience to catastrophic events in the future. Collectively, these recommendations are consistent with place-based conceptualizations of social vulnerability to disasters and are intended for implementation *before* the next large oil spill. The recommendations aim to build adaptive capacities and mitigate chronic stressors in communities experiencing disasters that impact the natural resources on which they rely.

Table 6.1. Summary of Recommendations

	Stakeholders with a Role in Addressing Each Recommendation					
Recommendation	Federal Government	State Government	Local Government	Non-governmental Organizations	Private Sector	Scientists
1. Focus on the needs of people and their communities.						
• Address acute needs (e.g., train and place community health workers to build local capacity for disaster response)	✓	✓	✓	✓		
• Ensure ongoing local support (e.g., provide sustained resources to local programs to address social disparities)			✓	✓	✓	
• Identify and support vulnerable populations (e.g., ensure that fishers have access to alternative livelihoods or income)			✓	✓	✓	✓

Recommendation	Stakeholders with a Role in Addressing Each Recommendation					
	Federal Government	State Government	Local Government	Non-governmental Organizations	Private Sector	Scientists
2. Address the complexity of the social systems in which disasters are managed.						
• Centralize social science in systems-based approaches to risk management (e.g., use citizen science to identify community assets for emergency response plans)	✓					✓
• Ensure that diverse information can be integrated by communities thinking holistically about their long-term needs and goals (e.g., provide funds to encourage communities to identify priority goals and strategies for achieving them)	✓	✓	✓	✓		✓
• Improve claims processes (e.g., clarify procedures in determining payouts ahead of the next disaster)	✓				✓	✓
3. Enhance partnerships, leveraging diverse sets of skills and strengths.						
• Work with local partners (e.g., engage residents in disaster citizen science)	✓	✓	✓	✓	✓	✓
• Leverage diverse skills to build systems-level capacity (e.g., use telemedicine to provide tailored, time-sensitive mental health care)	✓			✓		✓
• Integrate diverse perspectives through collaborations (e.g., enhance links between researchers and local residents through formal arrangements with community health workers)	✓	✓	✓	✓	✓	✓

Recommendation	Stakeholders with a Role in Addressing Each Recommendation					
	Federal Government	State Government	Local Government	Non-governmental Organizations	Private Sector	Scientists
4. Connect the past, present, and future contexts to support disaster recovery efforts						
• Examine extant policies and practices for ways to reduce vulnerabilities and increase resilience (e.g., identify potential hazardous waste disposal sites before the next disaster to distribute risk across sociodemographic groups)	✓	✓	✓	✓	✓	✓
• Improve adaptive capacity through preparedness and diversification (e.g., provide guidance to households about how to prepare for the mental, economic, and social distress associated with an oil spill)	✓	✓	✓		✓	
5. Deepen and communicate the evidence base for building community resilience						
• Partner with communities through participatory research approaches (e.g., partner with local organizations to design surveys and collect information)	✓			✓		✓
• Use prospective research designs, collect baseline data, and broaden the definition of *exposure* (e.g., include more social scientists on boards responsible for distributing research funds)	✓					✓
• Facilitate data sharing and access (e.g., coordinate research groups to avoid participant fatigue)	✓				✓	✓

Recommendation 1: Focus on the Needs of People and Their Communities

Public policies and practices around disaster planning, response, and recovery have disproportionately focused on biophysical issues (e.g., offsetting the risk of an oil spill with dispersants or engineered solutions). Despite the dominant role of place-based social attributes in determining disaster outcomes being well known to social scientists, people and their communities still tend not to be a central consideration in government approaches to dealing with disasters.[1] The small, but growing, body of empirical work on the human dimensions of the DWH oil spill demonstrates mixed evidence for mental health, economic, and community distress among residents along the northern Gulf Coast. The research points to multiple factors that affect people's vulnerability and resilience and highlights how different groups report different disaster experiences, even if they were not in physical contact with the oil. Therefore, the first recommendation focuses on ensuring that the needs of all local residents and their communities are understood and met, as needed, across the disaster life cycle.

Address Acute Needs

Government agencies at all levels (federal, state, and local) and nongovernment organizations play a primary role in addressing the acute needs of people and their communities. In the short term, resources are needed to address acute mental health symptoms, economic uncertainty and instability, and the interpersonal and community conflict that wears down social support networks. Two efforts have been made in this direction. First, the Resources and Ecosystems Sustainability, Tourist Opportunities, and Revived Economies of the Gulf Coast States Act (RESTORE Act), which was passed in 2012, established a Gulf Coast Restoration Trust Fund consisting of 80 percent of all administrative and civil penalties paid by the responsible parties for the oil spill. Second, the Gulf Region Health Outreach Program (GRHOP) was established with a portion of the medical claims settlement paid by BP to strengthen health care in Gulf Coast communities. One effort supported by GRHOP involved training community health workers and building local community capacity for future disaster responses. The extent to which these types of interventions are effective in improving the recovery processes for diverse local stakeholders requires in-depth evaluation.

Ensure Ongoing Local Support

In the medium to long term, support resources need to be sustained to address the chronic stress that individuals report experiencing and to strengthen various capacities in communities. Specifically, resources are needed to provide ongoing behavioral health services, especially for the most vulnerable members of the Gulf Coast population.[2] Local government, nongovernment

---

[1] Cope et al., 2013.

[2] Buttke, Vagi, Bayleyegn, et al., 2012; Buttke, Vagi, Schnall, et al., 2012b.

organizations, and the private sector are best positioned to provide such ongoing support. For instance, community health clinics, federally qualified community health care centers, and other providers in underserved areas know the types of behavioral health services their local residents need. They also know the exact nature and amount of resources required to provide these services appropriately. Other community nonprofits similarly know the long-term livelihood and social challenges being faced by individuals who are heavily dependent on natural resources when those resources are lost or threatened. Therefore, community development efforts should aim to sustain support for organizations working to enhance such attributes as community attachment to buffer against disaster impacts. Providing ongoing resources and guidance to local programs and smaller governing bodies before the next disaster occurs could help address social disparities and buffer against the breakdown of social support systems in times of intense stress.

Identify and Support Vulnerable Populations

More businesses, planners, resource managers, and elected officials need to recognize that some people are more likely than others to be affected with negative disaster outcomes and long-term consequences. In particular, in the context of environmental contamination, attention needs to be focused on the health, economic, and social needs of people, such as fishers, who have close ties to natural resources. In the event that individuals need to access programs that provide livelihood substitutions, the programs must be designed so that they are accessible even for community members with the most-limited resources. Other vulnerable groups identified in the research described in previous chapters include children, women, minorities, and those with less resources or less social support. One mechanism for this increased vulnerability relates to higher levels of stress or allostatic load.[3] Stakeholders with a primary role to play in implementing this recommendation include local government agencies, nongovernment organizations, and the private sector, with scientists supporting evidence-based decisions through their empirical work.

Recommendation 2: Address the Complexity of the Social Systems in Which Disasters Are Managed

The second recommendation is to address the complexity of the social systems in which disasters are managed. Although physical and natural scientists play a critical role in providing important technical information and insights, government is primarily responsible for leading response efforts, and public engagement is essential for the success of those efforts. However, public distrust in science, government, and private industry poses a barrier to effective engagement and risk communication.[4] The social, institutional, and political context is thus fundamental to the success of the work of resource managers and disaster responders. Failing to

---

[3] Chandra et al., 2018.

[4] Tuler and Kasperson, 2014.

understand and address these contextual factors can severely limit response and recovery for impacted communities. Risk management needs to be informed by social science that addresses the causes and consequences of disasters within these complex social systems.[5]

Centralize Social Science in Systems-Based Approaches to Risk Management

With the overarching role of guiding and coordinating efforts, the federal government (supported by scientific theory and empirical results) plays a primary role in ensuring that risk management considers the complex system in which disaster events occur and that social science is used to inform this understanding. Thinking of disasters within the context of social-ecological systems can help (1) avoid some of the unanticipated consequences that can arise as outputs of siloed interventions, (2) ensure that interventions address the multiple factors shaping risk, and (3) improve efficiencies by enhancing coordination.[6] For instance, disaster preparation and response plans that focus on only physical infrastructure (such as ensuring detailed maintenance protocols for oil rigs) will not address the health, economic, or community needs of impacted residents over time. A systems-based approach would consider ways in which vulnerability might be reduced in both physical infrastructure and local communities and how the two might interact. For instance, using citizen science to identify community assets for emergency response plans would increase residents' awareness of available infrastructure and the value of planning in case of disaster. Sandifer et al., 2017, provides a framework describing how human health, community environment, and sociodemographic characteristics interact to shape the health and economic impacts of oil spills. Such effects are not merely the additive result of each of these characteristics, but are instead the emergent outcome of the interaction among these characteristics.[7] This approach not only addresses physical or natural losses but also encourages investments in health, local economics, civic engagement, social ties, and functioning social services. This approach also recognizes that spill-related impacts and perceived impacts go far beyond the vicinity of the physically contaminated zone, affecting social and economic systems more broadly. Designing recovery efforts in a way that maintains and improves the well-being of impacted communities can help groups with few livelihood alternatives (e.g., fishers may not have the skills needed for oil and gas jobs that require the use of specific software)[8] and others (e.g., undocumented immigrants) who might be afraid to seek assistance.[9]

---

[5] Picou, Marshall, and Gill, 2004; Safford, Ulrich-Schad, and Hamilton, 2012; Finucane et al., 2019.

[6] Shultz et al., 2015.

[7] Wisner et al., 2004; Chaplin, Twigg, and Lovell, 2019.

[8] Gill, Picou, and Ritchie, 2012.

[9] Austin et al., 2014.

Improve Claims Processes

A unique aspect of technological disasters is that they are inevitably associated with complex litigation and compensation processes. Given that future technological disasters are inevitable, more-effective and -efficient forms of relief and restitution need to be developed.[10] This effort needs to be led by the federal government in partnership with the private sector and informed by health and social science that identifies the sources of—and methods for reducing—stress. The DWH claims process has been a clear secondary trauma for communities; the claims process became a new set of stressors, exacerbating the initial trauma and preexisting social disparities.[11] New relationships (e.g., dependence on government or a private actor for financial support), lack of clarity about the claims procedures, uncertainty about whether relief and restitution will result, and perceived ambiguity in decision processes or inequities in payout distributions, can lead to stress and community dysfunction. Social science is essential for assessing and addressing these stressors. Claims processes need to be improved in ways that reduce community infighting and allow people in the damaged areas more control over the recovery efforts. Particularly in communities that are heavily dependent on renewable resources, interventions that ameliorate resource disruption and build community connection could help promote resilience in a disaster context.[12]

Recommendation 3: Enhance Partnerships, Leveraging Diverse Sets of Skills and Strengths

The third recommendation is consistent with the Federal Emergency Management Agency's "whole of community" approach to disaster risk management, which underscores that everyone has a role in addressing disaster risk.[13]

Work with Local Partners

Interventions aimed at mitigating oil spill impacts must reflect people's unique place-based configuration of risk and resilience and be tailored to their local context.[14] In particular, efforts aimed at building community resilience (from planning to response and recovery) by government (at all levels), the private sector, and scientists must meaningfully incorporate and support local partners. The private sector in particular needs to establish strong, sustained local partnerships in advance of a crisis event so that local context is well understood and trusted relationships can be

---

[10] Ritchie, Gill, and Long, 2018.

[11] Mayer, Running, and Bergstrand, 2015.

[12] Parks et al., 2018; Abramson et al., 2015.

[13] Federal Emergency Management Agency, 2011.

[14] Finucane et al., 2019.

leveraged during difficult times. However, establishing partnerships between local and nonlocal groups might be challenging because of differences in groups' cultures, goals, and priorities.[15] Local government agencies and nongovernment organizations are particularly crucial partners because they have knowledge of local values and the expertise and capacity to operate in their environment.[16] However, local groups are sometimes marginalized from the recovery process, which often favors larger and more-formalized recovery organizations that are aligned with federal recovery organizational structures.[17] In addition, local groups often are overlooked in disaster planning processes within private organizations. Although local groups tend to be more agile than nonlocal groups because they operate at a smaller scale, they have more-limited economies of scale and fewer efficiencies than larger organizations. Accordingly, efforts should be made by federal agencies and private entities to strike a balance between the benefits that local organizations provide and their potential costs. Using citizen science during and after a disaster might be a promising way to enhance sustainable partnerships across disaster phases.[18]

Leverage Diverse Skills to Build Systems-Level Capacity

Diverse skills are needed to build capacity in systems targeting complex societal risks because of the multiple, interrelated dimensions of risk assessment, mitigation, and management processes. When diverse skills are leveraged effectively, there is more chance for enriched understanding of and solutions to risk management and societal outcomes. For instance, GRHOP is a partnership created from DWH oil spill settlement funds that aims to improve public health in the region. GRHOP leveraged the skills of communities, academics, and health providers through several activities designed to provide a systems-level recovery, by improving health care access, addressing mental health needs, and training health workers.[19] Because of its system orientation, GRHOP recognized the need to work collaboratively and involve many different organizations. One example effort aimed at meeting mental health needs after the DWH oil spill was GRHOP's Mental and Behavioral Health Capacity Projects. An initial assessment of the implementation of this project in Louisiana suggests that culturally tailored and time-sensitive services provided to adults and children onsite and via telemedicine resulted in reductions of mental health symptoms.[20] Stakeholders with a primary role in helping leverage diverse skills to build systems-level capacity are federal government agencies (e.g., the U.S. Department of

---

[15] Browne, 2015; Bankoff and Hilhorst, 2009; Hewitt, 2012.

[16] Lesen et al., 2019; Wilkinson, 2018; Browne and Olson, 2019.

[17] Lawther, 2009.

[18] Chari et al., 2019.

[19] Hansel et al., 2017.

[20] Osofsky, Osofsky, Wells et al., 2014.

Health and Human Services) and nonprofit organizations with broad interests or perspectives across sectors.

Integrate Diverse Perspectives Through Collaborations

To ensure that research and practice are relevant to the needs of diverse members of communities, collaborative approaches are important for ensuring that diverse perspectives are recognized, understood, and addressed. All stakeholders potentially play a role in collaborating, although primary responsibility likely depends on the purpose and availability of funding or other resources to support the efforts. For instance, the GoMRI-funded CRGC aims to assess and address the interlinked public health, social, and economic dimensions of the DWH oil spill by collaborating with many types of stakeholders, including researchers, health workers, and community groups.[21] One aspect of the CRGC program was to train community health workers with skills for enhancing disaster resilience.[22] In turn, the trainees provided important knowledge about networking with local residents, identifying priority concerns and stressors in their communities, and establishing the ground truth of early survey results. Consequently, CRGC was able to engage with communities that might have had less capacity to access resources or might have been more hesitant to seek out services, such as geographically isolated communities with limited transportation and undocumented communities. A similar approach could be adopted by private entities by providing the resources necessary for meaningful collaboration with local communities during the development of disaster planning, response, and recovery strategies.

Recommendation 4: Connect the Past, Present, and Future Contexts to Support Disaster Recovery Efforts

The fourth recommendation recognizes that oil spill disasters are not static, one-off events, but reflect vulnerabilities decades in the making, the outcomes of historical decisions that shape where people settle, the livelihoods in which they engage, and the resources that they can access.[23] Recovery efforts thus need to connect the past, present, and future contexts, working to reduce the underlying vulnerabilities that existed before the oil spilled occurred, addressing present needs across multiple domains, and building community capacities that create more resilience to disaster events in the future. Research and practice are increasingly recognizing the value of adaptive learning processes that address the dynamic linkages across time and across different types of decisionmakers.[24]

---

[21] Finucane et al., 2019.

[22] Nicholls, Picou, and McCord, 2017.

[23] Kwok, Engel, et al., 2017; Oliver-Smith, 2012; Oliver-Smith et al., 2017; Knowles, 2014; Morse, 2008; Ryder, 2017; Osofsky et al., 2012.

[24] Grannis, 2016; Klinke and Renn, 2012; Wardman and Mythen, 2016; Wilcox and Colwell, 2005.

Examine Extant Policies and Practices for Ways to Reduce Vulnerabilities and Increase Resilience

Disaster research and practice tends to focus on the immediate, near-term causes and consequences of disasters rather than the longer periods before or after the immediate emergency and recovery periods.[25] To understand the conditions that need to be addressed to reduce risk, policy and practice needs to be informed by historical and longitudinal analyses of how disasters emerge and evolve. For instance, the National Commission on the BP Deepwater Horizon Oil Spill and Offshore Drilling noted that, in the decades prior to the oil spill, environmental safeguards had eroded and oversight of the industry had become less effective as more demanding deep-water drilling was pursued in the Gulf of Mexico.[26] In addition, even though BP paid damages and contributed other resources, the burden of recovery tends to fall on state and local governments and their affected communities.[27] A simple step *before* the next oil spill would be to identify a variety of potential disposal sites for hazardous waste to prevent a disproportionate amount of the waste generated by a clean-up being allocated to sites near low-income communities of color.[28]

More broadly, research demonstrates that disaster impacts are unevenly spread because of preexisting socioeconomic conditions.[29] These and other factors shaping vulnerability (e.g., inequitable access to resources or employment opportunities) relate to broad social factors that are beyond the limited hazard-focused purview of disaster-management agencies. For instance, the exclusion of mental health problems from allowable claims from the Gulf Coast Compensation Fund made it harder for people with lower income to access needed services.[30] A longer-term perspective could inform ways in which funding structures (e.g., federal or private aid) could be modified to provide resources for resilience building before and after disasters (such as by including line items in government or corporate budgets). Incentives and policies for reducing "moral hazards" need to be considered to prevent the tendency to increase exposure to risk when someone else bears the costs of the risks (e.g., through insurance). All stakeholders would likely benefit from adopting a broader time perspective, but federal government agencies and scientists with relevant knowledge and resources may be particularly suited to implement this recommendation.

---

[25] Knowles, 2014; Oliver-Smith et al., 2016.

[26] National Commission on the BP Deepwater Horizon Oil Spill and Offshore Drilling, 2011.

[27] Chaplin, Twigg, and Lovell, 2019.

[28] Osofsky et al., 2012.

[29] Cutter, Boruff, and Shirley, 2003.

[30] Osofsky et al., 2012.

Adaptive capacity is the ability of a system to make long-term, sustainable adjustments to damage or transformation (abrupt or gradual) through novel organizational, technological, or other changes.[31] Adaptive and flexible interventions are crucial for responding to disaster impacts as they evolve over time. One way to support adaptive capacity is to establish contingency plans and mechanisms for task switching and scaling up and down to meet changing needs. *Preparedness* refers to the knowledge and capacities to address the impacts of disaster and helps communities rapidly transition between resource types during crisis.[32] Preparedness is particularly relevant for populations that experience disasters frequently—such as in the Gulf Coast region. However, although many communities know how to prepare for such natural hazards as hurricanes, they are less familiar with how to prepare for an oil spill. Disaster management agencies, including the Federal Emergency Management Agency and state and local agencies, offer relatively little guidance on what households and communities should do to prepare for oil spills. The lack of preparation is a mistake, given the rise of *natech* (processes defined by a combination of natural and technological hazards) disasters worldwide.[33] Beyond communicating about how to prevent or respond to physical exposure, efforts are needed to engage communities in thoughtful strategies for dealing with the array of mental, economic, and social distress potentially resulting from a disaster, such as a large oil spill. Stakeholders with a primary role include people responsible for planning or strategic thinking at all levels of government and the private sector. An important strategy for increasing adaptability and resilience is through economic diversification or opportunities for alternative livelihoods. When access to certain goods and services is disrupted, substitutability can be enhanced by investing in human and other sorts of capital that help reduce vulnerability. For instance, investments in vocational training and education programs could enhance the ability of workers to apply their skills in different sectors.

Recommendation 5: Deepen and Communicate the Evidence Base for Building Community Resilience

Scientific evidence about the human dimensions of oil spills needs to be developed. Compared with the extensive biophysical and ecological research, research on the human dimensions of oil spills is relatively scant. For instance, social scientists made up only 2 percent of the more than 1,200 students funded by GoMRI and human health–related research represents

---

[31] Adger, 2000; Gallopín, 2006.

[32] United Nations Office for Disaster Risk Reduction, undated; Federal Emergency Management Agency, 2018.

[33] Cruz and Suarez-Paba, 2019.

only 1 percent of oil spill studies conducted between 1968 and 2015.[34] Furthermore, only 4.2 percent of GoMRI's competitive grant funding was allocated to human dimensions (theme 5). This lack of support for human-focused research aligns with broader trends in disaster research, which is oriented primarily toward the biophysical rather than social dimensions of disaster.[35] Data that incorporate health, economic, and social outcomes over time in specific locations and socio-demographic contexts are rare. However, they provide insights about the specific types of stress or barriers encountered by some people that go well beyond generalities and thus allow for more-tailored interventions (e.g., telehealth may be more suited for people with pre-existing mental health conditions). Funding organizations need to develop and implement guidelines (in advance of the next disaster) for how to distribute and manage available funding and the other resources needed to expand and centralize social science in disaster research and practice. These guidelines should address (1) the disciplinary composition of review boards (to ensure that diverse social sciences are adequately represented) and (2) ways to hold funders accountable to a more-balanced distribution of resources across different disciplines. Assuming that adequate resources are provided for social science, the following recommendations provide suggestions for ways to strengthen empirical work aimed at enhancing community resilience.

Partner with Communities Through Participatory Research Approaches

To more rapidly improve how communities address risk, research needs to be developed in collaboration with potential end users throughout the research process.[36] This recommendation needs to be implemented primarily by federal agencies or other organizations providing research funding and members of the research community. Studies designed in ways that match community needs with useful outputs might be more effective in facilitating change within existing sociopolitical structures and processes.[37] Researchers can improve both data collection and engagement by partnering with local organizations. The CRGC efforts provide one example of how these partnerships could be structured. Drawing on semistructured exit interviews with CRGC partners on a survey project, Lesen and colleagues note that community collaborators considered partnership useful for collecting information on community needs and concerns.[38] One reason for the success of the CRGC collaborations was a longer engagement period that allowed for trust to be built. Also, community members learned that researchers were empathetic, while researchers learned how to conduct interviews using easily accessible terms and phrases. The authors argue that with these processes in place, community members can be

---

[34] Murphy et al., 2016.

[35] Cutter, Boruff, and Shirley, 2003.

[36] Wall, McNie, and Garfin, 2017.

[37] Lesen et al., 2019.

[38] Lesen et al., 2019.

powerful partners in research, both by acting as community brokers who facilitate connections between the research team and local community and by helping disseminate results to communities, including by holding researchers accountable to disseminate results.

Use Prospective Research Designs, Collect Baseline Data, and Broaden the Definition of "Exposure"

Disaster research is typically *reactive*, initiated only after a catastrophic event. As a result, prospective designs and baseline data are rare,[39] and causal analyses are undermined.[40] One reason for the reactive approach is that funding for research in this field tends to be responsive to disasters. Although time-sensitive research is necessary, funding for prospective designs is at least equally important. Research on oil spills is also challenging because of the complexity of the subject area, the difficult context for collecting data, and the challenges in accessing often marginalized and traumatized populations. A panel design that follows the same group of respondents over time would allow researchers to better track the dynamics of vulnerability and resilience to disaster impacts over time.[41] An additional problem is inconsistency in how "exposure" is conceived and operationalized. Lichtveld et al., for example, emphasizes how resilience among coastal workers and communities following the DWH oil spill was affected by chemical exposure and by nonchemical stressors,[42] while others focus on direct and indirect exposure elements.[43] These research issues are salient as we examine the long-term impacts of the oil spill and, as importantly, develop future mechanisms for integrating data developed during preparedness, response, and subsequent evaluations in other emergencies.[44] Social scientists with expertise on these issues need to be included more systematically in the boards responsible for reviewing research proposals and distributing funds. This recommendation could be implemented primarily by federal agencies or others funding research and by members of the research community.

Facilitate Data Sharing and Access

The DWH oil spill highlighted data sharing and access issues that need to be addressed. Although many government agencies collected population data, they could not always share it because of privacy and related issues.[45] Survey fatigue in many communities may have been

---

[39] Parker et al., 2019.

[40] Croisant et al., 2017.

[41] Parker et al., 2019.

[42] Lichtveld et al., 2016; Juarez et al., 2014; Vineis et al., 2017.

[43] Rung et al., 2017.

[44] Tierney, 2006.

[45] Fiore, Bond, and Nataraj, 2017.

avoided if engagement with different research groups could be minimized.[46] Access issues can be particularly salient for marginalized and vulnerable populations. Participation in the generation or consumption of research studies may be inhibited by linguistic and cultural differences. Collecting data from non-English speakers may be more difficult and there may be cultural disconnects between research teams and research participants that impact measure reliability or validity.[47] Science policy and practice should encourage research designs that address these limitations so that there are not systematic gaps regarding vulnerable populations in the body of empirical work being generated. Those with direct access to data—especially federal agencies, the private sector, and scientific organizations—need to shoulder primary responsibility for implementing this recommendation.

---

[46] Gulf Research Program, 2015.

[47] Lesen et al., 2019.

7. Conclusions

Ten years after the DWH oil spill, our synthesis of research suggests that evidence for mental health distress is mixed, with a lack of baseline data and prospective studies limiting the conclusions that can be made about causal linkages between the oil spill and mental health symptoms. Economic research suggests that impacts on commercial fisheries, seafood processing, and tourism were substantial but short-lived. Nonetheless, households reported experiencing negative financial stress associated with the oil spill. Finally, conditions following the oil spill suggest that communities faced chronic stressors, with some groups (e.g., fishers) appearing more vulnerable to social disruptions than others. Notably, only a small percentage of research funding awarded through competitive grant processes has been allocated to scientific studies of mental health, economic, or social aspects of the DWH oil spill.

Despite the limitations of research on mental health, economic, and community aspects of the DWH oil spill, specific recommendations for policy, practice, and research are apparent. A common theme emerging across the recommendations is that, in advance of another major oil spill, a sustained assessment and intervention process needs to be established to ensure that resources appropriately address acute and ongoing mental health, economic, and social well-being challenges in Gulf Coast communities. Social science needs to be central in this process to ensure a comprehensive understanding of and response to risk across the disaster life cycle. In particular, robust elicitation and integration of multiple perspectives on resilience are needed. Furthermore, evaluation and iterative adjustment of resilience-building efforts will provide nuanced information about what approaches are more suitable in different contexts. These recommendations are consistent with place-based conceptualizations of social vulnerability to disasters.

There are some aspects of the methods used to develop this report that necessarily limit the conclusions that can be made. First, papers in preparation or other work still in progress are not included and new evidence or insights may emerge in the near future that alter our understanding of mental health, economic, or community impacts of (and appropriate responses to) the DWH oil spill. Second, additional literature may have been overlooked because our search approach relied on Web of Science, PubMed, and other online databases specific to disasters or the DWH event and we did not systematically examine lessons from other oil spills (although some studies did compare DWH with the Exxon Valdez event).[1] Consequently, the recommendations in this report may not generalize to other contexts.

Nonetheless, the findings and recommendations presented in this report have value beyond the context of oil spills. Communities along the Gulf Coast and elsewhere face a variety of

---

[1] Gill, Picou, and Ritchie, 2012; Gill et al., 2014.

hazards, such as hurricanes, flooding, disease epidemics, and other events that can cause a heavy human toll. To be resilient, communities need to work together, developing and nurturing their assets and resources, understanding their collective and interdependent capacities to manage shocks and stressors, and investing in risk-reducing interventions. Although research and practice need to address the nuances of specific events and community characteristics, the key messages in this report underscore best practices for disaster management that are generalizable across contexts.

New information and insights on the human dimensions of the DWH oil spill will continue to emerge in the years to come. The new information will need to be synthesized and the lessons learned will need to be interpreted in the context of changing social-environmental conditions. New risks will exacerbate existing vulnerabilities and present difficult challenges for the mental health, quality of life, and rate of economic growth in Gulf Coast communities. To better inform policymakers and practitioners with evidence-based recommendations for building community resilience in the Gulf region, a broad coalition of stakeholders will need to develop and implement an ambitious, inclusive agenda of initiatives.

Appendix A. Report Methodology

This report integrated findings from a scoping literature review[1] and input from subject-matter experts. The literature review focused on articles about the mental health, economic, and community impacts of the DWH oil spill on Gulf Coast communities. To identify articles, we combined a topic search through Web of Science and PubMed with a review of other online databases specific to disasters or to the DWH oil spill. Web of Science and PubMed were used to identify academic literature, while the database review broadened the search and ensured collection of academic and grey literature. We searched "Deepwater Horizon" in Web of Science (returning 1,534 documents) and in PubMed (returning 783 documents). We reviewed other databases from websites, including research and policy organizations (e.g., Louisiana Public Health Initiative, Louisiana Oil Spill Coordinator's Office), research studies and consortia (e.g., The Transdisciplinary Research Consortium for Gulf Resilience on Women's Health, the Healthy Gulf, Healthy Communities Study), funders (e.g., Environmental Protection Agency, GoMRI), and online libraries (e.g., CRGC Resilient Gulf Resource Database, Natural Hazards Center Online Library Catalog). In total, we reviewed 20 databases and identified 4,268 documents. Combined with our Web of Science and PubMed searches, we identified a total of 6,540 items for review.

We reviewed the title and type of document of all identified articles to determine off-topic articles or non-research documents. Off-topic articles included articles on the ecological impacts of the oil spill, physical science, human impacts not related to the DWH oil spill, or only physical health impacts. Non-research articles included handouts, announcements, and other documents found mainly through the databases. A total of 6,386 off-topic or non-research documents were excluded.

We reviewed the abstract for each of the remaining 154 documents and excluded 39 documents deemed not relevant. Many of these documents had titles focused on the health impacts of the oil spill, but from reviewing the abstract, it became clear that the documents were discussing the physical or ecosystem health impacts of the oil spill. Subsequently, we reviewed each article in its entirety, excluding 17 articles that were off-topic, missing, or inaccessible. This process resulted in a final total of 98 documents for review (see Figure A.1). Each article was coded on the following dimensions: the impacts of the DWH oil spill on communities, including its mental health, economic, and social impacts; factors contributing to or inhibiting community resilience; gaps in knowledge; and potential ways to improve community resilience.

---

[1] Rumrill, Fitzgerald, and Merchant, 2010.

Figure A.1. Literature Review Selection Process

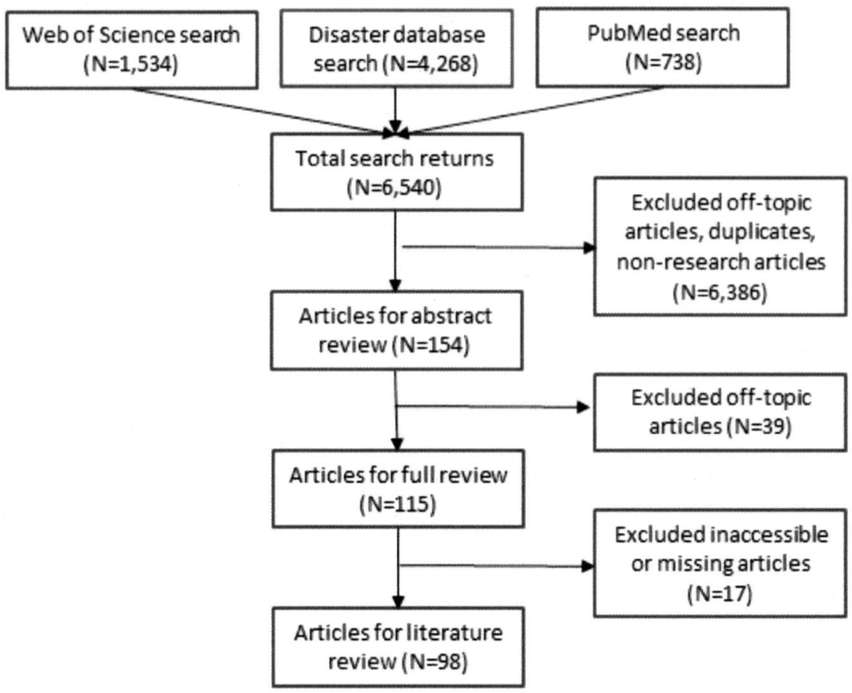

```
┌──────────────────┐  ┌──────────────────┐  ┌──────────────────┐
│ Web of Science   │  │ Disaster database│  │ PubMed search    │
│ search (N=1,534) │  │ search (N=4,268) │  │ (N=738)          │
└──────────────────┘  └──────────────────┘  └──────────────────┘
                  ↓        ↓        ↓
              ┌──────────────────┐              ┌──────────────────────┐
              │ Total search     │─────────────▶│ Excluded off-topic   │
              │ returns          │              │ articles, duplicates,│
              │ (N=6,540)        │              │ non-research articles│
              └──────────────────┘              │ (N=6,386)            │
                      ↓                          └──────────────────────┘
              ┌──────────────────┐              ┌──────────────────────┐
              │ Articles for     │─────────────▶│ Excluded off-topic   │
              │ abstract         │              │ articles (N=39)      │
              │ review (N=154)   │              └──────────────────────┘
              └──────────────────┘
                      ↓
              ┌──────────────────┐              ┌──────────────────────┐
              │ Articles for full│─────────────▶│ Excluded inaccessible│
              │ review           │              │ or missing articles  │
              │ (N=115)          │              │ (N=17)               │
              └──────────────────┘              └──────────────────────┘
                      ↓
              ┌──────────────────┐
              │ Articles for     │
              │ literature       │
              │ review (N=98)    │
              └──────────────────┘
```

The results of the literature review were coupled with feedback from the broader CRGC research team to draft our main findings on the health, economic, and community experiences associated with the DWH oil spill. The draft was presented at a one-day workshop designed to elicit feedback and identify high-level recommendations from subject-matter experts. The first half of the workshop was structured around presentations on the health, economic, and community dimensions of the oil spill. Each of these presentations focused on

- the top three findings
- the main gaps in knowledge
- three key recommendations.

Following each presentation, we elicited feedback on our results through a facilitated conversation with workshop participants focused on the following topics:

- If you wanted someone to take away just one thing from this work, what would that be?
- What strikes you as really important in this work?
- What gaps or needs still remain in this work?

The second half of the workshop focused on identifying the main overall messages and recommendations. Rather than presenting our own messages and recommendations, we elicited feedback from workshop participants on what they thought should be the main findings through three participatory exercises. The first exercise focused on identifying key overall messages, the second exercise focused on key recommendations, and the third exercise was designed to prioritize recommendations by ranking them on their impact and feasibility. At the start of each exercise, we divided the participants into two breakout groups to discuss the topic, then participants came together to compare discussion results and develop overall findings.

Participants were selected based on their knowledge of the impacts of the DWH oil spill and included academic researchers from a variety of disciplines and real-world practitioners who were responsible for providing support to communities during the oil spill. Participants included members of the CRGC research team (project investigators, associated researchers, and graduate students) and its stakeholder and technical advisory committees; disaster researchers and practitioners from GoMRI and external to GoMRI, including GRHOP; and nongovernment service providers. Approximately 25 people participated in the workshop.

The overall findings and recommendations that form the basis of this report were derived from the workshop discussions. A draft version of the report was shared with members of the CRGC team and workshop participants for review. Two independent peer reviewers (one external to RAND and one internal to RAND, neither of whom were associated with CRGC) also provided comments before the report was finalized.

Appendix B. Key Empirical Journal Articles and Other Reports Included for Review

Table B.1. Key Empirical Journal Articles and Other Reports Included for Review

Authors (Date)	Main Topic: Mental Health (MH), Economic (E), or Community (C)	Methods	Geographic Focus: Texas (TX), Louisiana (LA), Mississippi (MS), Alabama (AL), Florida (FL)	Year(s) Data Were Collected
Abramson et al. (2010)	MH	Probabilistic telephone survey	LA, MS	2010
Abramson et al. (2013)	MH	In-person household surveys	LA, MS, AL, FL	2012
Aiena et al. (2016)	MH	Patient questionnaires	MS	2010
Ayer et al. (2019)	MH	Probabilistic telephone survey	TX, LA, MS, AL, FL	2016
Bell, Langhinrichsen-Rohling, and Selwyn (2020)	MH	Purposive sampling, in-person survey	AL	2011
Bergstrand and Mayer (2017)	MH	Probabilistic telephone survey	AL, FL	2015
Buttke, Vagi, Bayleyegn, et al. (2012)	MH	Cluster sampling, in-person household surveys	MS, AL	2010
Buttke, Vagi, Schnall, et al. (2012)	MH	Cluster sampling, in-person household surveys	MS, AL	2011
Drescher, Schulenberg, and Smith (2014)	MH	In-person survey	MS	2011–2012
Fan et al. (2015)	MH	Representative telephone survey	LA, MS, AL, FL	2010–2011
Gould et al. (2015)	MH	Representative telephone survey	AL, FL, LA, MS	2010–2011
Grattan et al. (2011)	MH	In-person surveys	AL, FL	2010
Kwok et al. (2017)	MH	Prospective cohort	AL, FL, LA, MS, TX	2011–2013
Lee et al. (2019)	MH	Stratified, random sample, in-person survey	MS	2017
Morris et al. (2013)	MH	In-person interviews	AL, FL	2011–2012
Osofsky, Osofsky, and Hansel (2011)	MH	Random and purposive sampling, telephone and in-person interviews	LA	2010
Osofsky et al. (2014)	MH	Purposive sampling, patient questionnaires	LA	2013

Authors (Date)	Main Topic: Mental Health (MH), Economic (E), or Community (C)	Methods	Geographic Focus: Texas (TX), Louisiana (LA), Mississippi (MS), Alabama (AL), Florida (FL)	Year(s) Data Were Collected
Osofsky, Hansel, et al. (2015)	MH	Purposive sampling, telephone survey	LA	2011
Osofsky, Osofsky, et al. (2015)	MH	Multiwave, naturalistic design, in-person survey	LA	2009–2012
Ramchand et al. (2019)	MH	Probabilistic telephone survey	TX, LA, MS, AL, FL	2016
Shultz et al. (2015)	MH	Trauma signature analysis	Nonspecific	2010
Flocks and Davies (2014)	C	Focus groups, key informant interviews	AL, FL	2011–2013
Gill, Picou, and Ritchie (2012)	C	Probabilistic telephone survey	AL (and Alaska)	2010
Gill et al. (2014)	C	Probabilistic telephone survey	AL (and Alaska)	2011
Halmo, Griffith, and Stoffle (2019)	C	Ethnography	FL, AL, MS, LA	2016
Lesen et al. (2019)	C	Random and purposive sampling, interviews, in-person survey	LA, AL	2017
Mayer, Running, and Bergstrand (2015)	C	Focus groups, key informant interviews	AL, FL	2011–2013
Petrun-Sayers et al. (2019)	C	Probabilistic telephone survey	TX, LA, MS, AL, FL	2016
Ritchie, Gill, and Long (2018)	C	Probabilistic telephone survey	AL	2013
Safford et al. (2012)	C	Probabilistic telephone survey	LA, FL	2010
Sullivan, Ulrich-Schad, and Hamilton (2018)	C	Community-based participatory research	LA, MS, AL	2011
Aldy (2014)	E	Regression analysis using secondary data	TX, LA, MS, AL, FL	2010
Alvarez et al. (2014)	E	Site choice model using survey data	LA, MS, AL, GA, FL, SC, NC	2006–2010
Carroll et al. (2016)	E	Secondary data analysis	TX, LA, MS, AL, FL	2002–2013
English et al. (2018)	E	Site choice model using telephone survey data	Model focused on TX, LA, MS, AL, FL, GA; phone survey included individuals from continental United States	2012–2013
Fiore, Bond, and Nataraj (2019)	E	Regression analysis using secondary data	TX, LA, MS, AL, FL	2000–2015
Glasgow and Train (2018)	E	Adjustment factor for loss estimates	LA, MS, AL, Fl	2010–2011

Authors (Date)	Main Topic: Mental Health (MH), Economic (E), or Community (C)	Methods	Geographic Focus: Texas (TX), Louisiana (LA), Mississippi (MS), Alabama (AL), Florida (FL)	Year(s) Data Were Collected
Nadeau et al. (2014)	E	Mixed methods (claims data, interviews, year-over-year employment data)	LA, MS, AL, FL	2009–2011
Sumaila et al. (2012)	E	Modeling based on secondary data	TX, LA, MS, AL, FL	Various
U.S. Department of Commerce (2010)	E	Direct and indirect impacts of moratorium on drilling	TX, LA, MS, AL, FL	2010
Whitehead et al. (2018)	E	Travel cost estimate based on online survey	Estimate focused on FL; online survey included individuals from 13 states	2011
Austin et al. (2014)	C, E	Ethnography	LA, AL, MS	2010–2012
Cope et al. (2013)	MH, C	Repeated cross-sectional telephone survey	LA	2010, 2011, 2012, 2013
Cope et al. (2016)	MH, C	Repeated cross-sectional telephone survey	LA	2010, 2011, 2012, 2013
Cherry et al. (2015)	MH, C	Convenience samples, in-person survey	LA	Not specified
Cherry et al. (2017)	MH, C	Convenience samples, in-person survey	LA	Not specified
Gaston et al. (2017)	MH, C	U.S. Census data, convenience sample, telephone survey	LA	2012–2014, 2014–2016
Parks et al. (2018)	MH, C	Repeated cross-sectional telephone survey	LA	2010, 2011, 2012, 2013
Parks et al. (2019)	MH, C	Probabilistic telephone survey	TX, LA, MS, AL, FL	2016
Patel et al. (2018)	MH, C	Random and purposive sample, in-person surveys	LA, AL	2017
Rung et al. (2015)	MH, C, E	Convenience sample, telephone survey	LA	2011–2013
Rung et al. (2016)	MH, C, E	Population-based sample, telephone surveys	LA	2012–2014
Rung et al. (2017)	MH, C, E	Population-based sample, telephone surveys	LA	2012–2014
Shenesey and Langhinrichsen-Rohling (2015)	MH, C, E	Probabilistic telephone survey	AL	2011

Appendix C. Health, Economic, and Community Key Messages Presented at the Workshop

Key Messages: Health

Top Three Main Findings

1. The DWH oil spill may be associated with mental health distress.
2. There are many different causes of health problems.
3. Exposure to other shocks and stresses may exacerbate health problems.

Top Three Gaps in Knowledge

1. How should we define exposure?
2. What are the long-term population-wide public health impacts of oil spills?
3. How do oil spills affect the health of specific vulnerable populations?

Top Three Recommendations

1. Mental health services need to be provided over a long period.
2. Mental health support should be provided to a wide population group.
3. Targeted mental health outreach is needed.

Key Messages: Economic

Top Three Main Findings

1. The oil spill had negative short-term effects on commercial fisheries landings and on employment in some tourism industries.
2. There is little evidence of longer-term impacts on aggregate commercial fisheries or tourism metrics.
3. Losses in recreational activities were between 600 and 700 million dollars.

Top Three Gaps in Knowledge

1. Why were certain sectors more resilient than others?
2. How did the effects of the spill differ across individual fishers/businesses?
3. Are there policy interventions that could improve economic resilience?

Top Three Recommendations

1. Develop and disseminate better data to inform policy.
2. Establish processes for facilitating resilience when economic systems are compromised.
3. The public sector may need to provide short- and long-term support to help the economy.

Key Messages: Community

Top Three Main Findings

1. Gender and disaster exposure affected worry and risk perception.
2. Age, race, and education correlated with resilience.
3. Context and granularity is important.

Top Three Gaps in Knowledge

1. How do cumulative disasters affect households and communities?
2. How should households and communities prepare for oil spills?
3. How do different factors shape impact and recovery processes?

Top Three Recommendations

1. Policymakers should improve oil spill preparedness.
2. Interventions should be funded at the local level.
3. Responders should establish processes for maintaining community trust.

Bibliography

Abramson, David M., et al., *The Hurricane Sandy Place Report: Evacuation Decisions, Housing Issues and Sense of Community*, Rutgers University School of Social Work, New York University College of Global Public Health, Columbia University National Center for Disaster Preparedness, Colorado State University Center for Disaster and Risk Analysis, 2015.

Abramson, David M., Lori Ann Peek, Irwin E. Redlener, Jaishree Beedasy, Thomas Aguilar, Jonathan Sury, Akilah N. Banister, and Rebecca May, *Children's Health After the Oil Spill: A Four-State Study Findings from the Gulf Coast Population Impact (GCPI) Project*, New York: Columbia University, 2013.

Abramson, David M., Irwin E. Redlener, Tasha Stehling-Ariza, Jonathan Sury, Akilah N. Banister, and Yoon Soo Park, *Impact on Children and Families of the Deepwater Horizon Oil Spill: Preliminary Findings of the Coastal Population Impact Study*, New York: Columbia University, 2010.

Adger, W. Neil, "Social and Ecological Resilience: Are They Related?" *Progress in Human Geography*, Vol. 24, No. 3, 2000, pp. 347–364.

Aguilera, Francisco, Josefina Méndez, Eduardo Pásaro, and Blanca Laffon, "Review on the Effects of Exposure to Spilled Oils on Human Health," *Journal of Applied Toxicology*, Vol. 30, No. 4, 2010, pp. 291–301.

Aiena, Bethany J., Erin M. Buchanan, C. Veronica Smith, and Stefan E. Schulenberg, "Meaning, Resilience, and Traumatic Stress After the Deepwater Horizon Oil Spill: A Study of Mississippi Coastal Residents Seeking Mental Health Services," *Journal of Clinical Psychology*, Vol. 72, No. 12, 2016, pp. 1264–1278.

Aldy, Joseph E., *The Labor Market Impacts of the 2010 Deepwater Horizon Oil Spill and Offshore Oil Drilling Moratorium*, Cambridge, Mass.: National Bureau of Economic Research, 2014.

Alvarez, Sergio, Sherry L. Larkin, John C. Whitehead, and Tim Haab, "A Revealed Preference Approach to Valuing Non-Market Recreational Fishing Losses from the Deepwater Horizon Oil Spill," *Journal of Environmental Management*, Vol. 145, 2014, pp. 199–209.

Austin, Diane, Brian Marks, Kelly McClain, Tom McGuire, Ben McMahan, Victoria Phaneuf, Preetam Prakash, Bethany Rogers, Carolyn Ware, and Justina Whalen, *Offshore Oil and Deepwater Horizon: Social Effects on Gulf Coast Communities,* Vol. I, *Methodology,*

Timeline, Context, and Communities, New Orleans: Bureau of Ocean Energy Management, 2014.

Avery, Heidi, "The Ongoing Administration-Wide Response to the Deepwater BP Oil Spill," White House blog, May 5, 2010. As of June 8, 2020:
https://obamawhitehouse.archives.gov/blog/2010/05/05/ongoing-administration-wide-response-deepwater-bp-oil-spill

Ayer, Lynsey, Charles Engel, Andrew Parker, Rachana Seelam, and Rajeev Ramchand, "Behavioral Health of Gulf Coast Residents 6 Years After the Deepwater Horizon Oil Spill: The Role of Trauma History," *Disaster Medicine and Public Health Preparedness*, Vol. 13, No. 3, 2019, pp. 497–503.

Bankoff, Greg, and Dorothea Hilhorst, "The Politics of Risk in the Philippines: Comparing State and NGO Perceptions of Disaster Management," *Disasters*, Vol. 33, No. 4, 2009, pp. 686–704.

Barker, Kim, "'Spillionaires': Profiteering and Mismanagement in the Wake of the BP Oil Spill," *Propublica*, April 13, 2011. As of June 3, 2020:
https://www.propublica.org/article/spillionaires-profiteering-mismanagement-in-the-wake-of-the-bp-oil-spill

Bell, Tyler Reed, Jennifer Langhinrichsen-Rohling, and Candice N. Selwyn, "Conservation of Resources and Suicide Proneness After Oilrig Disaster," *Death Studies*, Vol. 44, No. 1, 2020, pp. 48–57.

Bergstrand, Kelly, and Brian Mayer, "Transformative Environmental Threats: Behavioral and Attitudinal Change Five Years After the Deepwater Horizon Oil Spill," *Environmental Sociology*, Vol. 3, No. 4, 2017, pp. 348–358.

Browne, Katherine E., *Standing in the Need: Culture, Comfort, and Coming Home After Katrina*, Austin: University of Texas Press, 2015.

Browne, Katherine E., and Laura Olson, *Building Cultures of Preparedness: A Report for the Emergency Management Higher Education Community*, Washington, D.C., Federal Emergency Management Agency, 2019.

Buttke, Danielle, Sara Vagi, Tesfaye Bayleyegn, Kanta Sircar, Tara Strine, Melissa Morrison, Mardi Allen, and Amy Wolkin, "Mental Health Needs Assessment After the Gulf Coast Oil Spill—Alabama and Mississippi, 2010," *Prehospital and Disaster Medicine*, Vol. 27, No. 5, 2012a, pp. 401–408.

Buttke, Danielle, Sara Vagi, Amy Schnall, Tesfaye Bayleyegn, Melissa Morrison, Mardi Allen, and Amy Wolki, "Community Assessment for Public Health Emergency Response

(CASPER) One Year Following the Gulf Coast Oil Spill: Alabama and Mississippi, 2011," *Prehospital and Disaster Medicine*, Vol. 27, No. 6, 2012b, pp. 496–502.

Carney, Diana, *Sustainable Rural Livelihoods: What Contribution Can We Make?* London: Department of International Deveopment, 1998.

Carroll, Michael, Brad Gentner, Sherry Larkin, Kate Quigley, Nicole Perlot, Lisa Dehner, and Andrea Kroetz, *An Analysis of the Impacts of the* Deepwater Horizon *Oil Spill on the Gulf of Mexico Seafood Industry*, Washington, D.C.: Bureau of Ocean Energy Management, 2016.

Chandra, Anita, Joie D. Acosta, Stefanie Howard, Lori Uscher-Pines, Malcolm V. Williams, Douglas Yeung, Jeffrey Garnett, and Lisa S. Meredith, *Building Community Resilience to Disasters: A Way Forward to Enhance National Health Security*, Santa Monica, Calif.: RAND Corporation, TR-915-DHHS, 2011. As of June 3, 2020:
https://www.rand.org/pubs/technical_reports/TR915.html

Chandra, Anita, Meagan Cahill, Douglas Yeung, and Rachel Ross, *Toward an Initial Conceptual Framework to Assess Community Allostatic Load: Early Themes from Literature Review and Community Analyses on the Role of Cumulative Community Stress*, Santa Monica, Calif.: RAND Corporation, RR-2559-RWJ, 2018. As of June 3, 2020:
https://www.rand.org/pubs/research_reports/RR2559.html

Chaplin, Daniel, John Twigg, and Emma Lovell, "Intersectional Approaches to Vulnerability Reduction and Resilience-Building," *Braced*, No. 12, April 2019.

Chari, Ramya, Marjory S. Blumenthal, and Luke J. Matthews, *Community Citizen Science: From Promise to Action*, Santa Monica, Calif.: RAND Corporation, RR-2763-RC, 2019. As of June 3, 2020:
https://www.rand.org/pubs/research_reports/RR2763.html

Chari, Ramya, Elizabeth L. Petrun Sayers, Sohaela Amiri, Mary Leinhos, Virginia Kotzias, Jaime Madrigano, Erin V. Thomas, Eric G. Carbone, and Lori Uscher-Pines, "Enhancing Community Preparedness: An Inventory and Analysis of Disaster Citizen Science Activities," *BMC Public Health*, Vol. 19, No. 1, 2019.

Cherry, Katie E., Laura Sampson, Sandro Galea, Loren D. Marks, Kayla H. Baudoin, Pamela F. Nezat, and Katie E. Stanko, "Health-Related Quality of Life in Older Coastal Residents After Multiple Disasters," *Disaster Medicine and Public Health Preparedness*, Vol. 11, No. 1, 2017, pp. 90–96.

Cherry, Katie E., Laura Sampson, Pamela F. Nezat, Ashley Cacamo, Loren D. Marks, and Sandro Galea, "Long-Term Psychological Outcomes in Older Adults After Disaster: Relationships to Religiosity and Social Support," *Aging and Mental Health*, Vol. 19, No. 5, 2015, pp. 430–443.

Clark-Ginsberg, Aaron, Leili Abolhassani, and Elahe Azam Rahmati, "Comparing Networked and Linear Risk Assessments: From Theory to Evidence," *International Journal of Disaster Risk Reduction*, Vol. 30, 2018, pp. 216–224.

Clark-Ginsberg, Aaron, and Rebecca Slayton, "Regulating Risks within Complex Sociotechnical Systems: Evidence from Critical Infrastructure Cybersecurity Standards," *Science and Public Policy*, Vol. 46, No. 3, 2018.

Cope, Michael R., Tim Slack, Troy C. Blanchard, and Matthew R. Lee, "Does Time Heal All Wounds? Community Attachment, Natural Resource Employment, and Health Impacts in the Wake of the BP Deepwater Horizon Disaster," *Social Science Research*, Vol. 42, No. 3, 2013, pp. 872–881.

———, "It's Not Whether You Win or Lose, It's How You Place the Blame: Shifting Perceptions of Recreancy in the Context of the Deepwater Horizon Oil Spill," *Rural Sociology*, Vol. 81, No. 3, 2016, pp. 295–315.

Croisant, Sharon A., et al., "The Gulf Coast Health Alliance: Health Risks Related to the Macondo Spill (GC-HARMS) Study: Self-Reported Health Effects," *International Journal of Environmental Research and Public Health*, Vol. 14, No. 11, 2017.

Cruz, Ana Maria, and Maria Camila Suarez-Paba, "Advances in Natech Research: An Overview," *Progress in Disaster Science*, Vol. 1, 2019.

Cutter, Susan L., "Vulnerability to Environmental Hazards," *Progress in Human Geography*, Vol. 20, No. 4, 1996, pp. 529–539.

Cutter, Susan L., Lindsey Barnes, Melissa Berry, Christopher Burton, Elijah Evans, Eric Tate, and Jennifer Webb, "A Place-Based Model for Understanding Community Resilience to Natural Disasters," *Global Environmental Change*, Vol. 18, No. 4, 2008, pp. 598–606.

Cutter, Susan L., Bryan J. Boruff, and W. Lynn Shirley, "Social Vulnerability to Environmental Hazards," *Social Science Quarterly*, Vol. 84, No. 2, 2003, pp. 242–261.

Drakeford, Leah, Vanessa Parks, Tim Slack, Rajeev Ramchand, Melissa Finucane, and Matthew R. Lee, "Oil Spill Disruption and Problem Drinking: Assessing the Impact of Religious Context Among Gulf Coast Residents," *Population Research and Policy Review*, Vol. 39, 2019, pp. 1–28.

Drescher, Christopher F., Stefan E. Schulenberg, and C. Veronica Smith, "The Deepwater Horizon Oil Spill and the Mississippi Gulf Coast: Mental Health in the Context of a Technological Disaster," *American Journal of Orthopsychiatry*, Vol. 84, No. 2, 2014, p. 142–151.

Eklund, Ruth L., Landon C. Knapp, Paul A. Sandifer, and Rita C. Colwell, "Oil Spills and Human Health: Contributions of the Gulf of Mexico Research Initiative," *GeoHealth*, Vol. 3, No. 12, 2019, pp. 391–406.

English, Eric, Roger H. von Haefen, Joseph Herriges, Christopher Leggett, Frank Lupi, Kenneth McConnell, Michael Welsh, Adam Domanski, and Norman Meade, "Estimating the Value of Lost Recreation Days from the Deepwater Horizon Oil Spill," *Journal of Environmental Economics and Management*, Vol. 91, 2018, pp. 26–45.

Erikson, K. T., *Everything in its Path*, New York: Simon and Schuster, 1976.

Fan, Amy Z., Marta R. Prescott, Guixiang Zhao, Carol A. Gotway, and Sandro Galea, "Individual and Community-Level Determinants of Mental and Physical Health After the Deepwater Horizon Oil Spill: Findings from the Gulf States Population Survey," *Journal of Behavioral Health Services and Research*, Vol. 42, No. 1, 2015, pp. 23–41.

Federal Emergency Management Agency, *A Whole Community Approach to Emergency Management: Principles, Themes, and Pathways for Action*, Washington, D.C., 2011.

———, *Federal Emergency Management Agency Strategic Plan*, Washington, D.C., 2018.

———, *Building Cultures of Preparedness: A Report for the Emergency Management Higher Education Community*, Washington, D.C., 2019.

Finucane, Melissa L., Michael J. Blum, Rajeev Ramchand, Andrew M. Parker, Shanthi Nataraj, Noreen Clancy, Gary Cecchine, Anita Chandra, Tim Slack, George Hobor, Regardt J. Ferreira, Ky Luu, Amy E. Lesen, and Craig A. Bond, "Advancing Community Resilience Research and Practice: Moving from 'Me' to 'We' to '3D,'" *Journal of Risk Research*, Vol. 23, No. 1, 2019, pp. 1–10.

Finucane, Melissa L., Noreen Clancy, Henry H. Willis, and Debra Knopman, *The Hurricane Sandy Rebuilding Task Force's Infrastructure Resilience Guidelines: An Initial Assessment of Implementation by Federal Agencies*, Santa Monica, Calif.: RAND Corporation, RR-841-DHS, 2014. As of June 3, 2020:
https://www.rand.org/pubs/research_reports/RR841.html

Fiore, Jacqueline, Craig A. Bond, and Shanthi Nataraj, *Estimating the Effects of the Deepwater Horizon Oil Spill on Fisheries Landings: A Preliminary Exploration*, Santa Monica, Calif.: RAND Corporation, WR-1173-GMA, 2017. As of June 3, 2020:
https://www.rand.org/pubs/working_papers/WR1173.html

———, *The Impact of the Deepwater Horizon Spill on Commercial Blue Crab Landings*, Santa Monica, Calif.: RAND Corporation, WR-1290-1-GMA, 2020. As of June 3, 2020:
https://www.rand.org/pubs/working_papers/WR1290-1.html

Flocks, Joan, and James Davies, "The *Deepwater Horizon* Disaster Compensation Process as Corrective Justice: Views from the Ground Up," *Mississippi Law Journal*, Vol. 84, No. 1, 2014, pp. 1–20.

Freudenburg, William R., "Risk and Recreancy: Weber, the Division of Labor, and the Rationality of Risk Perceptions," *Social Forces*, Vol. 71, No. 4, 1993, pp. 909–932.

Galea, Sandro, Andrea R. Maxwell, and Fran Norris, "Sampling and Design Challenges in Studying the Mental Health Consequences of Disasters," *International Journal of Methods Psychiatric Research*, Vol. 17, 2008, pp. S21–S28.

Gallopín, Gilberto C., "Linkages Between Vulnerability, Resilience, and Adaptive Capacity," *Global Environmental Change*, Vol. 16, No. 3, 2006, pp. 293–303.

Gaston, Symielle A., Julia Volaufova, Edward S. Peters, Tekeda F. Ferguson, William T. Robinson, Nicole Nugent, Edward J. Trapido, and Ariane L. Rung, "Individual-Level Exposure to Disaster, Neighborhood Environmental Characteristics, and Their Independent and Combined Associations with Depressive Symptoms in Women," *Social Psychiatry and Psychiatric Epidemiology*, Vol. 52, No. 9, 2017, pp. 1183–1194.

Gill, Duane A., and J. Steven Picou, "Technological Disaster and Chronic Community Stress," *Society and Natural Resources*, Vol. 11, No. 8, 1998, pp. 795–815.

Gill, Duane A., Steven Picou, and Liesel Ashley Ritchie, "The Exxon Valdez and BP Oil Spills: A Comparison of Initial Social and Psychological Impacts," *American Behavioral Scientist*, Vol. 56, No. 1, 2012, pp. 3–23.

Gill, Duane A., Liesel A. Ritchie, J. Steven Picou, Jennifer Langhinrichsen-Rohling, Michael A. Long, and Jessica W. Shenesey, "The Exxon and BP Oil Spills: A Comparison of Psychosocial Impacts," *Natural Hazards*, Vol. 74, No. 3, 2014, pp. 1911–1932.

Glasgow, Garrett, and Kenneth Train, "Lost Use-Value from Environmental Injury When Visitation Drops at Undamaged Sites," *Land Economics*, Vol. 94, No. 1, 2018, pp. 87–96.

Goldmann, Emily, and Sandro Galea, "Mental Health Consequences of Disasters," *Annual Review of Public Health*, Vol. 35, 2014, pp. 169–183.

Goldstein, Bernard D., Howard J. Osofsky, and Maureen Y. Lichtveld, "The Gulf Oil Spill," *New England Journal of Medicine*, Vol. 354, No. 14, 2011, pp. 1334–1348.

Gould, Deborah W., Judith L. Teich, Michael R. Pemberton, Carol Pierannunzi, and Sharon Larson, "Behavioral Health in the Gulf Coast Region Following the Deepwater Horizon Oil Spill: Findings from Two Federal Surveys," *Journal of Behavioral Health Services and Research*, Vol. 42, No. 1, 2015, pp. 6–22.

Grannis, Jessica, *Rebuilding with Resilience: Lessons from the Rebuild by Design Competition After Hurricane Sandy*, Washington, D.C.: Georgetown Climate Center, 2016.

Grattan, Lynn M., Sparkle Roberts, William T. Mahan, Jr., Patrick K. McLaughlin, W. Steven Otwell, and J. Glenn Morris, Jr., "The Early Psychological Impacts of the Deepwater Horizon Oil Spill on Florida and Alabama Communities," *Environmental Health Perspectives*, Vol. 119, No. 6, 2011, p. 838–843.

Gulf Research Program, *Opportunities for the Gulf Research Program: Community Resilience and Health: Summary of a Workshop*, Washington, D.C.: National Academies Press, 2015.

Hallman, W. K., and A. Wandersman, "Attribution of Responsibility and Individual and Collective Coping with Environmental Threats," *Journal of Social Issues*, Vol. 48, No. 4, 1992, pp. 101–118.

Halmo, David B., David Griffith, and Brent W. Stoffle, "'Out of Sight, Out of Mind': Rapid Ethnographic Assessment of Commercial Fishermen's Perspectives on Corporate/State Response to the Deepwater Horizon Disaster," *Human Organization*, Vol. 78, No. 1, 2019, pp. 1–11.

Hansel, T. C., et al., "Social and Environmental Justice as a Lens to Approach the Distribution of $105 Million of Directed Funding in Response to the Deepwater Horizon Oil Disaster," *Environmental Justice*, Vol. 10, No. 4, 2017, pp. 119–127.

Hansel, Tonya Cross, Howard J. Osofsky, Joy D. Osofsky, and Anthony Speier, "Longer-Term Mental and Behavioral Health Effects of the Deepwater Horizon Gulf Oil Spill," *Journal of Marine Science and Engineering*, Vol. 3, No. 4, 2015, pp. 1260–1271.

Harville, Emily W., Arti Shankar, Christine Dunkel Schetter, and Maureen Lichtveld, "Cumulative Effects of the Gulf Oil Spill and Other Disasters on Mental Health Among Reproductive-Aged Women: The Gulf Resilience on Women's Health Study," *Psychological Trauma: Theory, Research, Practice, and Policy*, Vol. 10, No. 5, 2018, p. 533–541.

Hewitt, K., "Culture, Hazard and Disaster," in Ben Wisner, J. C. Gaillard, and Ilan Kelman, eds., *The Routledge Handbook of Hazards and Disaster Risk Reduction*, London: Routledge, 2012, pp. 85–96.

Hobfoll, S. E., *The Ecology of Stress*, New York: Hemisphere, 1988.

———, "Conservation of Resources: A New Attempt at Conceptualizing Stress," *American Psychologist*, Vol. 44, No. 3, 1989, pp. 513–524.

Institute of Medicine, *Assessing the Effects of the Gulf of Mexico Oil Spill on Human Health: A Summary of the June 2010 Workshop*, Washington, D.C.: National Academies Press, 2010.

Juarez, Paul D., et al., "The Public Health Exposome: A Population-Based, Exposure Science Approach to Health Disparities Research," *International Journal of Environmental Research and Public Health*, Vol. 11, No. 12, 2014, pp. 12866–12895.

King, Lucy S., Joy D. Osofsky, Howard J. Osofsky, Carl F. Weems, Tonya C. Hansel, and Gregory M. Fassnacht, "Perceptions of Trauma and Loss Among Children and Adolescents Exposed to Disasters a Mixed-Methods Study," *Current Psychology*, Vol. 34, No. 3, 2015, pp. 524–536.

Klinke, Andreas, and Ortwin Renn, "Adaptive and Integrative Governance on Risk and Uncertainty," *Journal of Risk Research*, Vol. 15, No. 3, 2012, pp. 273–292.

Knowles, Scott Gabriel, "Learning from Disaster?: The History of Technology and the Future of Disaster Research," *Technology and Culture*, Vol. 55, No. 4, 2014, pp. 773–784.

Kwok, Richard K., Lawrence S. Engel, Aubrey K. Miller, Aaron Blair, Mattthew D. Curry, W. Braxton Jackson, Patricia A. Stewart, Mark R. Stenzel, Linda S. Birnbaum, Dale P. Sandler, and the GuLF Study Research Team, "The GuLF STUDY: A Prospective Study of Persons Involved in the *Deepwater Horizon* Oil Spill Response and Clean-Up," *Environmental Health Perspectives*, Vol. 125, No. 4, 2017, pp. 570–578.

Kwok, Richard K., John A. McGrath, Sarah R. Lowe, Lawrence S. Engel, W. Braxton Jackson, Matthew D. Curry, Julianne Payne, Sandro Galea, and Dale P. Sandler, "Mental Health Indicators Associated with Oil Spill Response and Clean-Up: Cross-Sectional Analysis of the GuLF STUDY Cohort," *Lancet Public Health*, Vol. 2, No. 12, 2017, pp. e560–e567.

Laffon, Blanca, Eduardo Pásaro, and Vanessa Valdiglesias, "Effects of Exposure to Oil Spills on Human Health: Updated Review," *Journal of Toxicology and Environmental Health, Part B*, Vol. 19, No. 3–4, 2016, pp. 105–128.

Larkin, Sherry L., Ray G. Huffaker, and Rodney L. Clouser, "Negative Externalities and Oil Spills: A Case for Reduced Brand Value to the State of Florida," *Journal of Agricultural and Applied Economics*, Vol. 45, 2013, pp. 389–399.

Lawther, Peter M., "Community Involvement in Post Disaster Re-Construction–Case Study of the British Red Cross Maldives Recovery Program," *International Journal of Strategic Property Management*, Vol. 13, No. 2, 2009, pp. 153–169.

Lee, Joohee, Bret J. Blackmon, Joo Young Lee, David M. Cochran, Jr., and Tim A. Rehner, "An Exploration of Posttraumatic Growth, Loneliness, Depression, Resilience, and Social Capital Among Survivors of Hurricane Katrina and the Deepwater Horizon Oil Spill," *Journal of Community Psychology*, Vol. 47, No. 2, 2019, pp. 356–370.

Lee, Matthew R., and Troy C. Blanchard, "Community Attachment and Negative Affective States in the Context of the BP *Deepwater Horizon* Disaster," *American Behavioral Scientist*, Vol. 56, No. 1, 2012, pp. 24–47.

Lesen, Amy E., Chloe Tucker, M. G. Olson, and Regardt J. Ferreira, "'Come Back at Us': Reflections on Researcher-Community Partnerships During a Post-Oil Spill Gulf Coast Resilience Study," *Social Sciences*, Vol. 8, No. 1, 2019, p. 8.

Lichtveld, Maureen, Samendra Sherchan, Kaitlyn B. Gam, Richard K. Kwok, Christopher Mundorf, Arti Shankar, and Lissa Soares, "The Deepwater Horizon Oil Spill Through the Lens of Human Health and the Ecosystem," *Current Environmental Health Reports*, Vol. 3, No. 4, 2016, pp. 370–378.

Loureiro, Maria L., Elena Ojea, Alfonso Ribas, and Edelmiro Lopez Iglesias, "Estimated Costs and Admissible Claims Linked to the Prestige Oil Spill," *Ecological Economics*, Vol. 59, No. 1, 2006, pp. 48–63.

Lowe, Sara R., Richard K. Kwok, Julianne Payne, Lawrence S. Engel, Sandro Galea, and Dale P. Sandler, "Mental Health Service Use by Clean-up Workers in The Aftermath of the Deepwater Horizon Oil Spill," *Social Science and Medicine*, Vol. 130, 2015, pp. 125–134.

———, "Why Does Disaster Recovery Work Influence Mental Health?: Pathways Through Physical Health and Household Income," *American Journal of Community Psychology*, Vol. 58, No. 3–4, 2016, pp. 354–364.

Mayer, Brian, Katrina Running, and Kelly Bergstrand, "Compensation and Community Corrosion: Perceived Inequalities, Social Comparisons, and Competition Following the Deepwater Horizon Oil Spill," *Sociological Forum*, Vol. 30, No. 2, June 2015, pp. 369–390.

McCormick, Sabrina, "After the Cap: Risk Assessment, Citizen Science and Disaster Recovery," *Ecology and Society*, Vol. 17, No. 4, 2012.

Michel, Jacqueline, Edward H. Owens, Scott Zengel, Andrew Graham, Zachary Nixon, Teresa Allard, William Holton, P. Doug Reimer, Alain Lamarche, Mark White, Nicolle Rutherford, Carl Childs, Gary Mauseth, Greg Challenger, and Elliott Taylor, "Extent and Degree of Shoreline Oiling: *Deepwater Horizon* Oil Spill, Gulf of Mexico, USA," *PLoS ONE*, Vol. 8, No. 6, 2013.

Morris, J. Glenn Jr., Lynn M. Grattan, Brian M. Mayer, and Jason K. Blackburn, "Psychological Responses and Resilience of People and Communities Impacted by the Deepwater Horizon Oil Spill," *Transactions of the American Clinical and Climatological Association*, Vol. 124, 2013, p. 191–201.

Morse, Reilly, *Environmental Justice Through the Eye of Hurricane Katrina*, Washington, D.C.: Joint Center for Political and Economic Studies, 2008.

Murphy, David, Brad Gemmell, Liana Vaccari, Cheng Li, Hernando Bacosa, Meredith Evans, Colbi Gemmell, Tracy Harvey, Maryam Jalali, and Tagbo H. R. Niepa, "An In-Depth Survey of the Oil Spill Literature Since 1968: Long Term Trends and Changes Since *Deepwater Horizon*," *Marine Pollution Bulletin*, Vol. 113, Nos. 1–2, 2016, pp. 371–379.

Nadeau, Lou, Maureen Kaplan, Melanie Sands, Katie Moore, and Charles Goodhue, *Assessing the Impacts of the* Deepwater Horizon *Oil Spill on Tourism in the Gulf of Mexico Region*, New Orleans: Bureau of Ocean Energy Management, 2014.

National Commission on the BP Deepwater Horizon Oil Spill and Offshore Drilling, *Deep Water: The Gulf Oil Disaster and the Future of Offshore Drilling*, Washington, D.C.: Oil Spill Commission, 2011.

National Oceanic and Atmospheric Association, "Deepwater Horizon Oil Spill Settlements: Where the Money Went," webpage, April 20, 2017. As of June 3, 2020:
https://www.noaa.gov/explainers/deepwater-horizon-oil-spill-settlements-where-money-went

National Wildlife Federation, "Deepwater Horizon's Impact on Wildlife," website, undated. As of June 8, 2020:
https://www.nwf.org/oilspill

Neria, Yuval, Anjali Nandi, and Sandro Galea, "Posttraumatic Stress Disorder Following Disasters: A Systematic Review," *Psychological Medicine*, Vol. 38, No. 4, 2008, pp. 467–480.

Ngo, D., J. L. Gibbons, G. Scire, and D. Le, "Mental Health Needs in Vietnamese American Communities Affected by the Gulf Oil Spill," *Psychology*, Vol. 5, No. 2, 2014, pp. 109–115.

Nicholls, Keith, Steven J. Picou, and Selena C. McCord, "Training Community Health Workers to Enhance Disaster Resilience," *Journal of Public Health Management and Practice*, Vol. 23, 2017, pp. S78–S84.

Norris, Fran H., Susan P. Stevens, Betty Pfefferbaum, Karen F. Wyche, and Rose L. Pfefferbaum, "Community Resilience as a Metaphor, Theory, Set of Capacities, and Strategy for Disaster Readiness," *American Journal of Community Psychology*, Vol. 41, Nos. 1–2, 2008, pp. 127–150.

Oliver-Smith, Anthony, "Anthropological Research on Hazards and Disasters," *Annual Review of Anthropology*, Vol. 25, 1996, pp. 303–328.

——— "Peru's Five-Hundred-Year Earthquake: Vulnerability in Historical Context," in Anthony Oliver-Smith and Susanna Hoffmann, eds., *The Angry Earth: Disaster in Anthropological Perspective*, Philadelphia: Taylor and Francis, 2012, pp. 88–102.

Oliver-Smith, Anthony, Irasema Alcántara-Ayala, Ian Burton, and Allan Lavell, *Forensic Investigations of Disasters (FORIN): A Conceptual Framework and Guide to Research*, Beijing: Integrated Research on Disaster Risk, 2016.

———, "The Social Construction of Disaster Risk: Seeking Root Causes," *International Journal of Disaster Risk Reduction*, Vol. 22, 2017, pp. 469–474.

Osofsky, Hari M., Kate Baxter-Kauf, Bradley Hammer, Ann Mailander, and Brett Mares, "Environmental Justice and the BP Deepwater Horizon Oil Spill," *New York University Environmental Law Journal*, Vol. 20, No. 1, 2012, pp. 99–198.

Osofsky, Howard J., Tonya Cross Hansel, Joy D. Osofsky, and Anthony Speier, "Factors Contributing to Mental and Physical Health Care in a Disaster-Prone Environment," *Behavioral Medicine*, Vol. 41, No. 3, 2015, pp. 131–137.

Osofsky, Howard J., Joy D. Osofsky, and Tonya C. Hansel, "Deepwater Horizon Oil Spill: Mental Health Effects on Residents in Heavily Affected Areas," *Disaster Medicine and Public Health Preparedness*, Vol. 5, No. 4, 2011, pp. 280–286.

Osofsky, Howard J., Joy D. Osofsky, John H. Wells, and Carl Weems, "Integrated Care: Meeting Mental Health Needs After the Gulf Oil Spill," *Psychiatric Services*, Vol. 65, No. 3, 2014, pp. 280–283.

Osofsky, Howard J., Lawrence A. Palinkas, and James M. Galloway, "Mental Health Effects of the Gulf Oil Spill," *Disaster Medicine and Public Health Preparedness*, Vol. 4, No. 4, 2010, pp. 273–276.

Osofsky, Joy D., Howard J. Osofsky, Carl F. Weems, Tonya C. Hansel, and Lucy S. King, "Effects of Stress Related to the Gulf Oil Spill on Child and Adolescent Mental Health," *Journal of Pediatric Psychology*, Vol. 41, No. 1, 2014, pp. 65–72.

Osofsky, Joy D., Howard J. Osofsky, Carl F. Weems, Lucy S. King, and Tonya C. Hansel, "Trajectories of Post-Traumatic Stress Disorder Symptoms Among Youth Exposed to Both Natural and Technological Disasters," *Journal of Child Psychology and Psychiatry*, Vol. 56, No. 12, 2015, pp. 1347–1355.

Palinkas, Lawrence A., "A Conceptual Framework for Understanding the Mental Health Impacts of Oil Spills: Lessons from the Exxon Valdez Oil Spill," *Psychiatry*, Vol. 75, No. 3, 2012, pp. 202–222.

Parker, Andrew M., Amanda F. Edelman, Katherine G. Carman, and Melissa L. Finucane, "On the Need for Prospective Disaster Survey Panels," *Disaster Medicine and Public Health Preparedness*, 2019, pp. 1–3.

Parker, Andrew M., Melissa L. Finucane, Lynsay Ayer, Rajeev Ramchand, Vanessa Parks, and Noreen Clancy, "Persistent Risk-Related Worry as a Function of Recalled Exposure to the

Deepwater Horizon Oil Spill and Prior Trauma," *Risk Analysis*, Vol. 40, No. 3, 2020, pp. 624–637.

Parks, Vanessa, Leah Drakeford, Michael R. Cope, and Tim Slack, "Disruption of Routine Behaviors Following the Deepwater Horizon Oil Spill," *Society and Natural Resources*, Vol. 31, No. 3, 2018, pp. 277–290.

Parks, Vanessa, Tim Slack, Rajeev Ramchand, Leah Drakeford, Melissa L. Finucane, and Matthew R. Lee, "Fishing Households, Social Support, and Depression After the Deepwater Horizon Oil Spill," *Rural Sociology*, Vol. 85, No. 2, 2019.

Patel, Megha M., Leia Y. Saltzman, Regardt J. Ferreira, and Amy E. Lesen, "Resilience: Examining the Impacts of the Deepwater Horizon Oil Spill on the Gulf Coast Vietnamese American Community," *Social Sciences*, Vol. 7, No. 10, 2018, p. 203.

Patel, Sonny S., M. Brooke Rogers, Richard Amlôt, and G. James Rubin, "What Do We Mean by 'Community Resilience'? A Systematic Literature Review of How It Is Defined in the Literature," *PLoS Currents Disasters*, Vol. 9, 2017.

Peres, Lauren C., Edward Trapido, Ariane L. Rung, Daniel J. Harrington, Evrim Oral, Zhide Fang, Elizabeth Fontham, and Edward S. Peters, "The Deepwater Horizon Oil Spill and Physical Health Among Adult Women in Southern Louisiana: The Women and Their Children's Health (WaTCH) Study," *Environmental Health Perspectives*, Vol. 124, No. 8, 2016, p. 1208–1213.

Perry, R. W., and E. L. Quarantelli, *What Is a Disaster? New Answers to Old Questions*, Philadelphia: Xlibris, 2005.

Petrun Sayers, Elizabeth L., Andrew M. Parker, Rajeev Ramchand, Melissa L. Finucane, Vanessa Parks, and Rachana Seelam, "Reaching Vulnerable Populations in the Disaster-Prone US Gulf Coast: Communicating Across the Crisis Lifecycle," *Journal of Emergency Management*, Vol. 17, No. 4, 2019, pp. 271–286.

Picou, J. Steven, Brent K. Marshall, and Duane A. Gill, "Disaster, Litigation, and the Corrosive Community," *Social Forces*, Vol. 82, No. 4, 2004, pp. 1493–1522.

Quarantelli, E. L., "Conceptualizing Disasters from a Sociological Perspective," *International Journal of Mass Emergencies and Disasters*, Vol. 7, No. 3, 1989, pp. 243–251.

———, "A Social Science Research Agenda for the Disasters of the Twenty-First Century: Theoretical, Methodological and Empirical Issues and Their Professional Implementation," in E. L. Quarantelli, ed., *What Is a Disaster? New Answers to Old Questions*, Philadelphia: Xlibris, 2005, pp. 325–396.

Ramchand, Rajeev, Rachana Seelam, Vanessa Parks, Bonnie Ghosh-Dastidar, Matthew R Lee, and Melissa Finucane, "Exposure to the Deepwater Horizon Oil Spill, Associated Resource

Loss, and Long-Term Mental and Behavioral Outcomes," *Disaster Medicine and Public Health Preparedness*, Vol. 13, No. 5–6, 2019, pp. 889–897.

Ritchie, Liesel A., Duane A. Gill, and Michael A. Long, "Mitigating Litigating: An Examination of Psychosocial Impacts of Compensation Processes Associated with the 2010 BP *Deepwater Horizon* Oil Spill," *Risk Analysis*, Vol. 38, No. 8, 2018, pp. 1656–1671.

Rumrill, Phillip D., Shawn M. Fitzgerald, and William R. Merchant, "Using Scoping Literature Reviews as a Means of Understanding and Interpreting Existing Literature," *Work*, Vol. 35, No. 3, 2010, pp. 399–404.

Rung, Ariane L., Symielle Gaston, Evrim Oral, William T. Robinson, Elizabeth Fontham, Daniel J. Harrington, Edward Trapido, and Edward S. Peters, "Depression, Mental Distress, and Domestic Conflict Among Louisiana Women Exposed to the *Deepwater Horizon* Oil Spill in the WaTCH Study," *Environmental Health Perspectives*, Vol. 124, No. 9, 2016, pp. 1429–1435.

Rung, Ariane L., Symielle Gaston, William T. Robinson, Edward J. Trapido, and Edward S. Peters, "Untangling the Disaster-Depression Knot: The Role of Social Ties After Deepwater Horizon," *Social Science Medicine*, Vol. 177, No. 1, 2017, pp. 19–26.

Rung, Ariane L., Evrim Oral, Elizabeth Fontham, Daniel J. Harrington, Edward J. Trapido, and Edward S. Peters, "Mental Health Impact of the Deepwater Horizon Oil Spill Among Wives of Clean-Up Workers," *Epidemiology*, Vol. 26, No. 4, 2015.

Ryder, Stacia S., "A Bridge to Challenging Environmental Inequality: Intersectionality, Environmental Justice, and Disaster Vulnerability," *Social Thought and Research*, Vol. 34, 2017, pp. 85–115.

Safford, Thomas G., Jessica D. Ulrich-Schad, and Lawrence C. Hamilton, "Public Perceptions of the Response to the Deepwater Horizon Oil Spill: Personal Experiences, Information Sources, and Social Context," *Journal of Environmental Management*, Vol. 113, 2012, pp. 31–39.

Sandifer, Paul A., Landon C. Knapp, Tracy K. Collier, Amanda L. Jones, Robert-Paul Juster, Christopher R. Kelble, Richard K. Kwok, John V. Miglarese, Lawrence A. Palinkas, Dwayne E. Porter, Geoffrey I. Scott, Lisa M. Smith, William C. Sullivan, and Ariana E. Sutton-Grier, "A Conceptual Model to Assess Stress-Associated Health Effects of Multiple Ecosystem Services Degraded by Disaster Events in the Gulf of Mexico and Elsewhere," *GeoHealth*, Vol. 1, No. 1, 2017, pp. 17–36.

Sandifer, Paul A., and Ann Hayward Walker, "Enhancing Disaster Resilience by Reducing Stress-Associated Health Impacts," *Frontiers in Public Health*, Vol. 6, 2018, p. 373.

Shenesey, Jessica W. and Jennifer Langhinrichsen-Rohling, "Perceived Resilience: Examining Impacts of the Deepwater Horizon Oil Spill One-Year Post-Spill," *Psychological Trauma: Theory, Research, Practice, and Policy*, Vol. 7, No. 3, 2015, pp. 252–258.

Shultz, James M., Lauren Walsh, Dana Rose Garfin, Fiona E. Wilson, and Yuval Neria, "The 2010 Deepwater Horizon Oil Spill: The Trauma Signature of an Ecological Disaster," *Journal of Behavioral Health Services and Research*, Vol. 42, No. 1, 2015, pp. 58–76.

Simon-Friedt, Bridget R., Jessi L. Howard, Mark J. Wilson, David Gauthe, Donald Bogen, Daniel Nguyen, Ericka Frahm, and Jeffrey K. Wickliffe, "Louisiana Residents' Self-Reported Lack of Information Following the Deepwater Horizon Oil Spill: Effects on Seafood Consumption and Risk Perception," *Journal of Environmental Management*, Vol. 180, 2016, pp. 526–537.

Singleton, B., J. Turner, L. Walter, N. Lathan, D. Thorpe, P. Ogbevoen, J. Daye, D. Alcorn, S. Wilson, J. Semien, T. Richard, T. Johnson, K. McCabe, J. J. Estrada, F. Galvez, C. Velasco, and K. Reiss, "Environmental Stress in the Gulf of Mexico and Its Potential Impact on Public Health," *Environmental Research*, Vol. 146, 2016, pp. 108–115.

Strelitz, Jean, Lawrence S. Engel, Richard K. Kwok, Aubrey K. Miller, Aaron Blair, and Dale P. Sandler, "Deepwater Horizon Oil Spill Exposures and Nonfatal Myocardial Infarction in the GuLF STUDY," *Environmental Health*, Vol. 17, No. 1, 2018.

Sullivan, J., et al., "Building and Maintaining a Citizen Science Network with Fishermen and Fishing Communities Post Deepwater Horizon Oil Disaster Using a CBPR Approach," *New Solutions: A Journal of Environmental and Occupational Health Policy*, Vol. 28, No. 3, 2018, pp. 416–447.

Sumaila, U. Rashid, Andrés M. Cisneros-Montemayor, Andrew Dyck, Ling Huang, William Cheung, Jennifer Jacquet, Kristin Kleisner, Vicky Lam, Ashley McCrea-Strub, Wilf Swartz, Reg Watson, Dirk Zeller, and Daniel Pauly, "Impact of the Deepwater Horizon Well Blowout on the Economics of U.S. Gulf Fisheries," *Canadian Journal of Fisheries and Aquatic Sciences*, Vol. 69, No. 3, 2012, pp. 499–510.

Tierney, Kathleen, "Social Inequality, Hazards, and Disasters," in R. J. Daniels, D. F. Kettl, and H. Kunreuther, eds., *Risk and Disaster: Lessons from Hurricane Katrina*, Philadelphia: University of Pennsylvania Press, 2006, pp. 109–127.

Tuler, Seth P. and Roger E. Kasperson, "Social Distrust and Its Implications for Risk Communication: An Example from High Level Radioactive Waste Management," in Joseph Arvai and Louie Rivers III, eds., *Effective Risk Communication*, Routledge: London, 2014.

United Nations Office for Disaster Risk Reduction, "Terminology," webpage, undated. As of June 3, 2020:
https://www.preventionweb.net/terminology

Upton, Harold F., *The Deepwater Horizon Oil Spill and the Gulf of Mexico Fishing Industry*, Washington, D.C.: Congressional Research Service, 7-5700, February 17, 2011.

U.S. Coast Guard and National Response Team, *On Scene Coordinator Report: Deepwater Horizon Oil Spill*, Washington, D.C.: U.S. Department of Homeland Security and U.S. Coast Guard, 2011.

U.S. Department of Commerce, *Estimating the Economic Effects of the Deepwater Drilling Moratorium on the Gulf Coast Economy: Inter-Agency Economic Report*, Washington, D.C., 2010.

U.S. Environmental Protection Agency, "Summary of Criminal Prosecutions," website, 2013. As of June 3, 2020:
http://cfpub.epa.gov/compliance/criminal_prosecution/index.cfm?action=3&prosecution_summary_id=2468

Vineis, P., et al., "The Exposome in Practice: Design of the EXPOsOMICS Project," *International Journal of Hygiene and Environmental Health*, Vol. 220, No. 2, 2017, pp. 142–151.

Wall, Tamara U., Elizabeth McNie, and Gregg M. Garfin, "Use-Inspired Science: Making Science Usable by and Useful to Decision Makers," *Frontiers in Ecology and the Environment*, Vol. 15, No. 10, 2017, pp. 551–559.

Wardman, Jamie K., and Gabe Mythen, "Risk Communication: Against the Gods or Against All Odds? Problems and Prospects of Accounting for Black Swans," *Journal of Risk Research*, Vol. 19, No. 10, 2016, pp. 1220–1230.

Whitehead, John C., Tim Haab, Sherry L. Larkin, John B. Loomis, Sergio Alvarez, and Andrew Ropicki, "Estimating Lost Recreational Use Values of Visitors to Northwest Florida due to the Deepwater Horizon Oil Spill Using Cancelled Trip Data," *Marine Resource Economics*, Vol. 33, No. 2, 2018, pp. 119–132.

Wilcox, Bruce A., and Rita R. Colwell, "Emerging and Reemerging Infectious Diseases: Biocomplexity as an Interdisciplinary Paradigm," *EcoHealth*, Vol. 2, No. 244, 2005.

Wilkinson, Olivia, "'Faith Can Come in, but Not Religion': Secularity and Its Effects on the Disaster Response to Typhoon Haiyan," *Disasters*, Vol. 42, No. 3, 2018, pp. 459–474.

Wisner, Ben, Piers Blaikie, Terry Cannon, and Ian Davis, *At Risk: Natural Hazards, People's Vulnerability and Disasters*, New York: Routledge, 2004.